Spring Boot Messaging

Messaging APIs for Enterprise and Integration Solutions

Felipe Gutierrez

Apress®

Spring Boot Messaging: Messaging APIs for Enterprise and Integration Solutions

Felipe Gutierrez
Albuquerque, New Mexico, USA

ISBN-13 (pbk): 978-1-4842-1225-7   ISBN-13 (electronic): 978-1-4842-1224-0
DOI 10.1007/978-1-4842-1224-0

Library of Congress Control Number: 2017941320

Managing Director: Welmoed Spahr
Editorial Director: Todd Green
Acquisitions Editor: Steve Anglin
Development Editor: Matthew Moodie
Technical Reviewer: Manuel Jordan Elera
Coordinating Editor: Mark Powers
Copy Editor: Kezia Endsley
Compositor: SPi Global
Indexer: SPi Global
Artist: SPi Global
Cover image designed by Freepik

Distributed to the book trade worldwide by Springer Science+Business Media New York, 233 Spring Street, 6th Floor, New York, NY 10013. Phone 1-800-SPRINGER, fax (201) 348-4505, e-mail orders-ny@springer-sbm.com, or visit www.springeronline.com. Apress Media, LLC is a California LLC and the sole member (owner) is Springer Science + Business Media Finance Inc (SSBM Finance Inc). SSBM Finance Inc is a **Delaware** corporation.

For information on translations, please e-mail rights@apress.com, or visit http://www.apress.com/rights-permissions.

Apress titles may be purchased in bulk for academic, corporate, or promotional use. eBook versions and licenses are also available for most titles. For more information, reference our Print and eBook Bulk Sales web page at http://www.apress.com/bulk-sales.

Any source code or other supplementary material referenced by the author in this book is available to readers on GitHub via the book's product page, located at www.apress.com/9781484212257. For more detailed information, please visit http://www.apress.com/source-code.

Printed on acid-free paper

To my daughter, Laura Gutierrez

Contents at a Glance

About the Author xiii

About the Technical Reviewer xv

Acknowledgments xvii

■Chapter 1: Messaging 1

■Chapter 2: Spring Boot 7

■Chapter 3: Application Events 17

■Chapter 4: JMS with Spring Boot 31

■Chapter 5: AMQP with Spring Boot 59

■Chapter 6: Messaging with Redis 81

■Chapter 7: Web Messaging 93

■Chapter 8: Messaging with Spring Integration 111

■Chapter 9: Messaging with Spring Cloud Stream 133

■Chapter 10: Reactive Messaging 163

■Chapter 11: Microservices 179

Index 193

Contents

About the Author xiii

About the Technical Reviewer xv

Acknowledgments xvii

■Chapter 1: Messaging.. 1

Messaging.. 1

Messaging Use Cases... 1

Messaging Models and Messaging Patterns... 3

Messaging with Spring Framework 5

Summary.. 5

■Chapter 2: Spring Boot 7

What Is Spring Boot?... 7

Spring Boot's Features 7

Restful API with Spring Boot 8

The rest-api-demo Project.. 8

Running the Spring Boot Currency Web App.. 15

Deploying the Spring Boot Currency Web App 15

More About Spring Boot 15

Summary.. 16

■Chapter 3: Application Events 17

The Observer Pattern 17

The Spring ApplicationEvent 18

Spring ApplicationListener 19

Rest API Currency Project 20

    Custom Events 23

Using Event Listeners with Annotations 27

    @EventListener 27

    @TransactionalEventListener 29

Summary 30

■Chapter 4: JMS with Spring Boot 31

JMS 31

    JMS with Java 32

JMS with Spring Boot 36

    Producer 36

    Consumer 38

    Consumer with Annotations 42

    Currency Project 43

    Reply-To 51

    Topics 54

Currency Project 57

Summary 57

■Chapter 5: AMQP with Spring Boot 59

The AMQP Model 59

    Exchanges, Bindings, and Queues 60

RabbitMQ 62

RabbitMQ with Spring Boot 62

    Producer 63

    Consumer 67

    RPC 70

    Reply Management 75

    Flow Control 76

More Features 78

Currency Project 80

Summary 80

■**Chapter 6: Messaging with Redis** **81**

Redis as a Message Broker 81

Publish/Subscribe Messaging with Redis 83

Subscriber 83

Publisher 86

JSON Serialization 88

The Currency Project 92

Summary 92

■**Chapter 7: Web Messaging** **93**

WebSockets 93

Using WebSockets with Spring 94

Low-Level WebSockets 94

Using SockJS and STOMP 101

Using RabbitMQ as a STOMP Broker Relay 108

Currency Project 109

Summary 110

■**Chapter 8: Messaging with Spring Integration** **111**

Spring Integration Primer 112

Programming Spring Integration 113

A Simple Spring Integration Example 114

File Integration Example 121

File and JDBC Integration Example 124

AMQP Integration Example 128

Currency Exchange Project 131

Summary 131

■**Chapter 9: Messaging with Spring Cloud Stream**..**133**

Spring Cloud.. 133

Spring Cloud Stream 134

    Spring Cloud Stream Concepts.. 135

Spring Cloud Stream Programming... 136

    cloud-stream-demo.. 139

    Microservices 154

Spring Cloud Stream App Starters 160

    source:http 160

    sink:log 160

Currency Project 162

What's Next? 162

Summary... 162

■**Chapter 10: Reactive Messaging** **163**

Reactive Programming.. 163

RxJava... 164

    The rxjava-demo Project... 164

Reactor.. 170

    The reactor-demo Project.. 170

Spring 5: WebFlux Framework 173

    Programming Models 173

Summary... 178

■**Chapter 11: Microservices** **179**

What Microservices Are 179

The Twelve Factor Apps.. 180

Spring Cloud Services 182

Spring Cloud Config Server 182

Service Registry 184

Circuit Breaker 190

About Reactive Programming 192

Summary 192

Index 193

About the Author

Felipe Gutierrez is a solutions software architect, with bachelor's and master's degrees in computer science from Instituto Tecnologico y de Estudios Superiores de Monterrey Campus Ciudad de Mexico. Gutierrez has over 20 years of IT experience and has developed programs for companies in multiple vertical industries, such as government, retail, healthcare, education, and banking. Right now, he is currently working as a principal technical instructor for Pivotal, specializing in Cloud Foundry, Spring Framework, Spring Cloud Native Applications, Groovy, and RabbitMQ, among other technologies. He has worked as a solutions architect for big companies like Nokia, Apple, Redbox, and Qualcomm, and others. He is also the author of *Introducing Spring Framework and Pro Spring Boot,* published by Apress Media, LLC.

About the Technical Reviewer

Manuel Jordan Elera is an autodidactic developer and researcher who enjoys learning new technologies for his own experiments and creating new integrations.

Manuel won the Springy Award – Community Champion and Spring Champion 2013. In his little free time, he reads the Bible and composes music on his guitar. Manuel is known as dr_pompeii. He has tech reviewed numerous books for Apress, including *Pro Spring, 4th Edition* (2014), *Practical Spring LDAP* (2013), *Pro JPA 2, Second Edition* (2013), and *Pro Spring Security* (2013).

Read his 13 detailed tutorials about many Spring technologies, contact him through his blog at http://www.manueljordanelera. blogspot.com, and follow him on his Twitter account, @dr_pompeii.

Acknowledgments

I would like to express all my gratitude to the Apress team—to Steve Anglin for accepting my proposal, to Mark Powers for keeping me on track and for his patience with me, and to the rest of the Apress team involved in this project. Thanks to everybody for making this possible.

Thanks to my technical reviewer, Manuel Jordan, for all the detail and effort in his reviews, and the entire Spring team for creating this amazing technology.

Thanks to my wife Norma Castaneda for her love and support. Thanks to my girls—Laura, Nayely, Ximena—and my baby Rodrigo! Thanks to my parents, Rocio Cruz and Felipe Gutierrez, my brother Edgar Gerardo Gutierrez, and my sister-in-law Auristella Sanchez for her love and support.

—Felipe Gutierrez

## CHAPTER 1

Messaging

Communication is a concept that has been around forever. Everything needs to communicate by exchanging some kind of information, and yes, you read that right, I mean *everything*. If you think about it, even the ads that you find on the side of a bus or in the grocery store are trying to tell or sell you something, right?

In the computer world, devices (mouse, monitor, keyboard, etc.) communicate with each other by exchanging bits of information. If we consider applications, then we are talking about components, functions, classes, etc., that need to communicate with each other or expose some functionality that can be reached through communication. We typically call this *messaging*.

Messaging

This section introduces some of the main concepts described in detail later, starting with messaging and how it fits in the daily development cycle. Take a look at Figure 1-1.

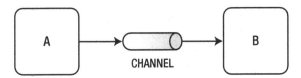

Figure 1-1. *Messaging*

Figure 1-1 shows a simple messaging process, whereby it communicates from point A to point B through whatever media is possible. In this case, Figure 1-1 uses a channel, which could be a simple function call, a socket connection, or an HTTP request. The main idea is to produce/send a message to the consumer/receiver.

Messaging Use Cases

This section covers some of the most common messaging use cases. These uses cases are key to understanding why messaging is so important:

- *Delivery Guaranteed*

  - Developers need to make sure that the message they are sending reaches its destination. If you are using a *broker* (a system that handles connections, messages, and message delivery, synched or asynched), then the producer needs to know if the broker receives the message, by some kind of acknowledgement. The consumer must do the same, by acknowledging to the broker that the message was received. So this particular use case is commonly used when critical messages are being delivered, such as payments, stocks, or any other important information.

- *Decoupled*

  - When dealing with software architecture, developers look for decoupled components for easy integration, extensibility, and simple operation and maintenance. But how can you achieve decoupling? Messaging is part of the solution, because it allows you to think in your own business domain, which is a bounded context. The information you produce/send is your main concern, regardless of how the consumer/receiver will implement its own business logic.

- *Scalable and High Available*

  - Every time a system experiences high-request demands, it needs to be scalable and not have a single point of failure. For these particular scenarios, messaging is the solution, because multiple consumers/receivers can keep up with the load and you can replicate the messages across multiple system instances or brokers. That way, if one of your instances/brokers is down, you are still in control.

- *Asynchronous*

  - Applications must be very quick and be able to respond to a request as soon as possible. In this case, time is the key factor. How can you achieve this kind of speed when you know that processing the request will take a lot of time and you have multiple clients? You can solve this issue by using the previous use case solution (scalability and/or high availability), but it will reach a point where it's blocking requests. The solution is asynchronous messaging—a fire and forget—where your producer/sender sends messages and gets to their own business logic, leaving the consumers/receivers to process the message on their own time.

- *Interoperability*

  - An important factor when creating messaging systems is the ability to produce/send a message and be able to understand that message when consuming/receiving (maybe it's a plain/text JSON or in XML format or a serialized object). There have been many attempts over the past decades to create interoperable systems. Nowadays, interoperability is possible with new brokers like the one that implements the AMQP protocol or even with simple RESTful APIs or WebSockets that, regardless of the implementation, enable the producer and consumer to interoperate seamlessly.

These use cases have been evolving into very well known messaging models and design patterns, which are discussed in the next section.

Messaging Models and Messaging Patterns

Some messaging models were established when messaging became a part of all systems. These models, in my opinion, evolved into the creation of messaging design patterns.

Point-to-Point

A point-to-point model is a way to send a message to a queue (First In, First Out), whereby only one receiver gets the message. See Figure 1-2.

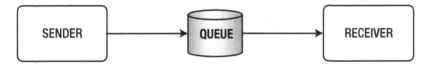

Figure 1-2. *Point-to-point model*

The point-to-point model is also used as a message channel pattern, whereby instead of a queue, you have a channel (which is a way to transport your message). It still guarantees that only one receiver gets the message in the order it was sent.

You'll see some examples later in the book about these models and patterns.

Publish-Subscribe

The publish-subscribe model describes a publisher that sends a message (a topic) to multiple subscribers of that topic. Each subscriber will receive only one copy of the message. See Figure 1-3.

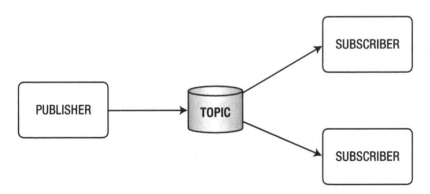

Figure 1-3. *Publish–subscribe model*

The publish-subscribe model is also used as a message channel pattern, whereby instead of a topic, you have a channel that delivers a copy of the message to its subscribers.

These models are more related to the JMS (Java Messaging System) and are important to understand because they form the basics of all enterprise systems.

Messaging Patterns

A design pattern is a solution to a commonly known problem in the software design. By the same token, messaging patterns attempt to solve problems with messaging designs.

You will learn about the implementation of the following patterns during the course of this book, so I want to list them here with simple definitions to introduce them:

- *Message type patterns*: Describe different forms of messaging, such as string (maybe plain text, JSON and/or XML), byte array, object, etc.

- *Message channel patterns*: Determine what kind of a transport (channel) will be used to send a message and what kind of attributes it will have. The idea here is that the producer and consumer know how to connect to the transport (channel) and can send and receive the message. Possible attributes of this transport include a request-reply feature and a unidirectional channel, which you will learn about very soon. One example of this pattern is the point-to-point channel.

- *Routing patterns*: Describe a way to send messages between producer and consumers by providing a routing mechanism (filtering that's dependent on a set of conditions) in an integrated solution. That can be accomplished by programming, or in some cases, the messaging system (the broker) can have these capabilities (as with RabbitMQ).

- *Service consumer patterns*: Describe how the consumers will behave when messages arrive, such as adding a transactional approach when processing the message. There are frameworks that allow you to initiate this kind of behavior (like the Spring Framework, which you do by adding the @ Transactional, a transaction-based abstraction).

- *Contract patterns*: Contracts between the producer and consumer to have simple communications, such as when you do some REST calls, where you call a JSON or XML message with some fields.

- *Message construction patterns*: Describe how a message is created so it can travel within the messaging system. For example, you can create an "envelope" that can have a body (the actual message) and some headers (with a correlation ID or a sequence or maybe a reply address). With a simple web request, you can add parameters or headers and the actual message becomes the body of the request, making the whole request part of the construction pattern. The HTTP protocol allows for that kind of communication (messaging).

- *Transformation patterns*: Describe how to change the content of the message within the messaging system. Think about a message that requires some processing and needs to be enhanced on the fly, such as a content enricher.

As you can see, these patterns not only describe the messaging process but some of them describe how to handle some of the common use cases you saw earlier. Of course, there are a lot more messaging patterns, and these are just a few that we are going to explore in this book.

If you want more information, I recommend that you visit the Enterprise Integration Patterns web site, `http://www.enterpriseintegrationpatterns.com/`. Also check out this must-read book—*Enterprise Integration Patterns: Designing, Building, and Deploying Messaging Solutions* by Gregor Hohpe and Bobby Woolf, from Addison-Wesley.

In the book, I cover some of these patterns using the Spring Integration module and various messaging systems (brokers).

Messaging with Spring Framework

The Spring Framework is one of the most commonly used frameworks by the Java community. The Spring Framework has enabled a simple and easy way to do messaging, by implementing a template design pattern that can be used with any messaging system. It supports the JMS API with the JmsTemplate, the AMQP with the RabbitTemplate, STOMP, and internal messaging with events and listeners. Don't worry, we will cover all of these later in book.

It's worth mentioning that the Spring Integration project has been well accepted by the community, and the core of the Spring Integration (messaging, channels, and other interfaces) has been part of the Spring Core since version 4.0.

There are many good messaging frameworks out there. Some of them use pure Java, and others depend on the Spring Framework. The Spring team has been working very hard to make it even easier for its developers to use all the features, including concurrency, transactions, retries, etc. To use other libraries, you have to implement them by hand using the same logic.

■ **Note**   You can download the book's source code from the Apress site or you can clone it from this GitHub repository: `https://github.com/felipeg48/spring-messaging`.

Summary

This chapter introduced messaging and the messaging systems. You read about the basic concept of messaging, whereby developers need to send information from one point to another.

The chapter reviewed some use cases, models, and patterns of messaging. The book will cover them in more detail and use them via some of the best implementations out there, including the Spring Framework and some of their modules, including Spring Integration, Spring AMQP, and Spring Cloud Stream.

The next chapter includes a tour of Spring Boot, which is the next generation of creating enterprise-ready Spring applications. Spring Boot is the base for all the modules you use in this book.

CHAPTER 2

Spring Boot

I'll start with a phrase that I wrote in another book: *Spring Boot is a new chapter in creating enterprise-ready applications with the Spring Framework.*

Spring Boot does not replace the Spring Framework; you can see it as a new way to create awesome applications with the framework used by the Java community.

In this chapter, I show you what Spring Boot is and how it works behind the scenes. You will also see the power of Spring Boot with a small example. So why do we need to look at Spring Boot? First of all, all the technologies that we are going to use, such as Spring Integration, Spring AMQP, Spring Cloud Stream, and others, use Spring Boot as their base. All the examples in this book use Spring Boot to create Spring apps. And of course, Spring Boot makes messaging even easier.

What Is Spring Boot?

To begin with, Spring Boot is an *opinionated* technology. What does that mean?

Spring Boot looks at the classpath and tries to determine what kind of application you are trying to run. For example, if you have the `spring-mvc` modules in your classpath, Spring Boot will wire up the `WebApplicationInitializer` and `DispatcherServlet` classes inside the Spring container and will set up an embedded container (Tomcat by default), so you can run your application without having to copy or deploy your application to a servlet container.

Spring Boot's Features

Let's look at the most important Spring Boot features:

- It can create standalone Spring applications. Based on its Maven or Gradle plugin, you can create executable JARs or WARs.

- It has an opinionated technology based on the *starter* poms.

- Includes auto-configuration, which will configure your Spring application without any XML or Java config classes.

- Includes embedded servlet containers for web apps (Tomcat, Jetty, or Undertow).

- Includes production-ready features (non-functional requirements) that are ready to use, such as metrics and health checks.

© Felipe Gutierrez 2017
F. Gutierrez, *Spring Boot Messaging*, DOI 10.1007/978-1-4842-1224-0_2

- Spring Boot *is not* a plugin or a code generator (this means that Spring Boot doesn't create a file to be compiled).

- If you have an application or servlet container, you can deploy Spring Boot as a WAR without making any changes.

- You can access all the Spring application events and listeners (something that we will discuss in the next chapter).

This list is just a few features of what Spring Boot can offer; of course there are more. I recommend my other book—*Pro Spring Boot* from Apress—if you need to know more about it. That book includes more comprehensive and detailed sections about how Spring Boot works internally.

Restful API with Spring Boot

One of the important features of Spring Boot is that you can create executable JARs and run them by just executing `java -jar yourapp.jar`. You can also create executable WARs (web archive) that can run standalone (using the embedded container within the WAR) or deploy them to a servlet container without chaining anything in your code.

This section shows you a Restful API that lists the currency and the rates based on the country code. This project is a Spring Boot web application.

■ **Note** You can find a download link for all the source code at the `http://www.apress.com/9781484212257`.

I'll show you some code snippets of the application, so you have an idea of what Spring Boot can do with very minimal code and no configuration files.

I'm assuming that you already have the code. I suggest that you use the STS (Spring Tool Suite), which you can get from `https://spring.io/tools/sts/all`. I use this IDE because it has very nice features for running Spring Boot, and all the figures that you see are based on this IDE, but you can choose any IDE you like.

The rest-api-demo Project

This project is a Spring Boot web application that will expose Restful endpoints that will show a country currency and the rates of other countries. This project is in the folder named ch02.

This project also uses the JPA (Java Persistence API) with an in-memory database (using the H2 engine), AOP (Aspect-Oriented Programming). The exposed endpoints are listed in Table 2-1.

Table 2-1. *Restful Endpoints*

Method	Path	Description
GET	/currency/latest[?base=<code>]	Shows the latest rates in JSON format. USD is the default base.
GET	/currency/{date}[?base=<code>]	Shows the rates based on the date: yyyy-MM-dd in JSON format.
GET	/currency/{amount}/{base}/to/{code}	Shows a conversion based on the amount, base, and code.
POST	/currency/new	Adds new rates by date. The body should be in JSON format.

Listing 2-1 shows an example of the JSON response. You can use a base parameter for some of the endpoints as well.

Listing 2-1. JSON Currency Response - /currency/latest

```
{
    "base": "USD",
    "date": "2016-09-22",
    "rates": [
        {
            "code": "EUR",
            "rate": 0.88857
        },
        {
            "code": "JPY",
            "rate": 102.17
        },
        {
            "code": "MXN",
            "rate": 19.232
        },
        {
            "code": "GBP",
            "rate": 0.75705
        }
    ]
}
```

Listing 2-1 shows you the result response by accessing the /currency/latest endpoint. It shows the base currency, in this case the U.S. Dollar, and all the rates (currency) that you can get from the other countries with 1 USD.

For a conversion, you request the endpoint /currency/{amount}/{base}/to/{code}. Imagine you want to know how many Japanese Yens are equal to 10 USD. The request can be done like this: /currency/10/usd/to/jpy. You should get the result shown in Listing 2-2.

Listing 2-2. Conversion Response - /currency/10/usd/to/jpy

```
{
    "base": "USD",
    "code": "JPY",
    "amount": 10.0,
    "total": 1021.69995
}
```

Listing 2-2 shows you the result of the conversion endpoint. Let's review the other files.

The pom.xml File

Open the pom.xml file and review its contents. Let's review the tags and their meanings:

- The <packaging/> tag has the WAR value. When packaging this application, it will generate a WAR that will be executable and deployable to any servlet container.

  ```
  <packaging>war</packaging>
  ```

- The <parent/> tag is the key for Spring Boot to work, because it has all the dependencies and versions that you need in your application. It is based on Maven's BOM (Bill of Materials) feature. So, it is important that this particular tag always be in your Spring Boot application.

  ```
  <parent>
      <groupId>org.springframework.boot</groupId>
      <artifactId>spring-boot-starter-parent</artifactId>
      <version>1.4.0.RELEASE</version>
      <relativePath /> <!-- lookup parent from repository -->
  </parent>
  ```

- The <dependencies/> tag holds all the dependencies in the Spring Boot application. When you choose the web dependency (using the command line or the Spring starter), the spring-boot-web-starter dependency is added to this pom. This is similar to when you selected the project as a WAR type, whereby the spring-boot-starter-tomcat dependency was added. By default, you always have the spring-boot-starter-test dependency.

  ```
  <dependencies>
      <dependency>
          <groupId>org.springframework.boot</groupId>
          <artifactId>spring-boot-starter-web</artifactId>
      </dependency>
  ```

```xml
        <dependency>
            <groupId>org.springframework.boot</groupId>
            <artifactId>spring-boot-starter-tomcat</artifactId>
            <scope>provided</scope>
        </dependency>
        <dependency>
            <groupId>org.springframework.boot</groupId>
            <artifactId>spring-boot-starter-data-jpa</artifactId>
        </dependency>
        <dependency>
            <groupId>com.h2database</groupId>
            <artifactId>h2</artifactId>
            <scope>runtime</scope>
        </dependency>
        <dependency>
            <groupId>org.springframework.boot</groupId>
            <artifactId>spring-boot-starter-aop</artifactId>
        </dependency>
        <dependency>
            <groupId>org.springframework.boot</groupId>
            <artifactId>spring-boot-starter-test</artifactId>
            <scope>test</scope>
        </dependency>
    </dependencies>
```

Let's take a moment to look at the <dependencies/> tag. If you are familiar with the Maven way to create a project, you will figure this out by now, that there is a missing tag in the <dependency/> tag. That's right, the <version/> tag is missing. This version is not used any more because the <parent/> tag definition includes all the versions and dependencies that you will use in your web application.

Notice that spring-boot-starter-tomcat has the scope as provided, which means you can create a runnable WAR (that you can run using java -jar <war-name>.war) and deploy it to any servlet container.

Notice the naming convention that you use to create Spring Boot apps—every <groupId/> tag is org.springframework.boot and the <artifactId/> tag is spring-boot-starter-<technology>.

Why is this important? Remember that Spring Boot is an opinionated technology, so based on this pom and the spring-boot-starter, it will recognize which application you are trying to run.

The Rate.java Class

This will be the domain class. It includes an annotation that defines it as an entity. This is because this class will be persisted into the H2 engine (in-memory database). See Listing 2-3.

Listing 2-3. src/main/java/com/apress/messaging/domain/Rate.java

```java
@Entity
public class Rate {

        @Id
        private String code;
        private Float rate;

        @JsonIgnore
        @Temporal(TemporalType.DATE)
        private Date date;

        // Setters and Getters omitted.

}
```

Listing 2-3 shows you the domain class—here the @Entity and @Id annotations are being used—and this is related to the JPA technology (Spring Data JPA). As you can see, it's very basic. Nothing too complicated.

The RateRepository.java Class

Next is the RateRepository interface, which is based on the Spring Data JPA technology, where you need to extend from the JpaRepository<E,ID> and add the entity (domain) and the ID class type (String, a serializable class) that will be used for persistence. See Listing 2-4.

Listing 2-4. src/main/java/com/apress/messaging/repository/RateRepository.java

```java
@Repository
public interface RateRepository  extends JpaRepository<Rate,String>{
        List<Rate> findByDate(Date date);
        Rate findByDateAndCode(Date date,String code);
}
```

Listing 2-4 shows you the RateRepository interface. You can see the @Repository annotation (this is just a marker for the Spring container); the important part is that you need to extend from the JpaRepository interface. This interface will implement all the *CRUD* (Create, Read, Update and Delete) actions for you, so you don't have to implement them. Two query methods are defined—findByDate (looks for the rates that have that date) and findByDateAndCode (looks for a specific date and code). What makes this interface special is that you can create a SQL query by using the properties of the domain class. If you want to learn more about Spring Data JPA, go to http://docs.spring.io/spring-data/jpa/docs/current/reference/html/.

The CurrencyController.java Class

This class defines the REST endpoints. It uses the RateRepository interface through a service. See Listing 2-5.

Listing 2-5. src/main/java/com/apress/messaging/controller/CurrencyController.java

```
@RestController
@RequestMapping("/currency")
public class CurrencyController {

    @Autowired
    CurrencyConversionService service;

    @RequestMapping("/latest")
    public ResponseEntity<CurrencyExchange> getLatest(@RequestParam(name="base",
    defaultValue=CurrencyExchange.BASE_CODE)String base) throws Exception{
            //...
    }

    @RequestMapping("/{amount}/{base}/to/{code}")
    public ResponseEntity<CurrencyConversion> conversion(@PathVariable("amount")
    Float amount,@PathVariable("base")String base,@PathVariable("code")String code)
    throws Exception{
            //...
    }

    //More methods here...

}
```

Listing 2-5 shows you a snippet of the CurrencyController class, which uses the Spring MVC @RestController, @RequestMapping, @RequestParam, and @PathVariable annotations. Every response is based on the ResponseEntity class.

This is pure Spring MVC (not too much Spring Boot). If you want to know more about Spring MVC, visit http://docs.spring.io/spring/docs/current/spring-framework-reference/html/mvc.html.

Review this class and experiment with it.

The RestApiDemoApplication.java Class

This class is the main entry point of the web application. See Listing 2-6.

Listing 2-6. src/main/java/com/apress/messaging/RestApiDemoApplication.java

```
@SpringBootApplication
public class RestApiDemoApplication {

    public static void main(String[] args) {
      SpringApplication.run(RestApiDemoApplication.class, args);
    }

    @Bean
    public CommandLineRunner data(RateRepository repository) {
      return (args) -> {
          repository.save(new Rate("EUR",0.88857F,new Date()));
          repository.save(new Rate("JPY",102.17F,new Date()));
          repository.save(new Rate("MXN",19.232F,new Date()));
          repository.save(new Rate("GBP",0.75705F,new Date()));
        };
    }
}
```

Listing 2-6 shows you the main class, where Spring Boot will bootstrap the application. @SpringBootApplication is a required annotation for every Spring Boot app, because it will trigger all the magic behind Spring Boot. This annotation will use the *auto-configuration* feature to determine your app and the best configuration for it. In this case, because you have the spring-boot-starter-web dependency (in your classpath through your pom.xml file), it will set up all the necessary beans (like the DispatcherServlet) and the embedded servlet container (Tomcat by default) to configure your web app.

Notice the @Bean, which returns a CommandLineRunner interface. This will be executed after the Spring container is ready with all your beans, and it will use the RateRepository interface to save the rate. You can see this as a way to initialize your database.

Other Files...

Of course, there are more classes, but the idea here is for you to experiment with them and see what they do and how they are used in the project. Look at the CurrencyConversionService class, which is used in the web controller.

If you want to see how the AOP is being used in this project, look at the CurrencyCodeAudit class. It's defining an around advice that will be executed only when an @ToUpper annotation is found in a method. (You can get the code from this annotation in the book's source code.) Why do you need to use this aspect? Well, if you look at the conversion endpoint, you are expecting a capital case (for the base and the code, /150/USD/to/JPY), but with this approach, you can ignore it. Removing @ToUpper from the CurrencyConversionService methods, such as /150/usd/to/jpy, doesn't work, because it's evaluating just the capital letters for the base and code. You instead need to add extra code to support it.

Running the Spring Boot Currency Web App

There are different ways to run a project like this. If you use the STS and import the project, you can simply right-click the project's name and choose Run As --> Spring Boot App, and that's it!

If you want to run it using the command line, make sure you have Maven installed and execute:

```
$ mvn spring-boot:run
```

Then you can go to your browser and type http://localhost:8080/currency/latest and you should get the same result as shown in Listing 2-1. You can also use the curl command:

```
$ curl http://localhost:8080/currency/latest
```

As you can see, you don't need to create a WAR and deploy it to a container, because Spring Boot comes with an embedded Tomcat container. This allows you to have portability.

Deploying the Spring Boot Currency Web App

If you want to deploy this code to a servlet container, you need to package this project. If you are using the STS, you can right-click over the project and select Run As --> Maven Build. This will bring up a dialog box. In the Goals field, enter Package and then check the Skip Test check box. You can then click Run. This will create an executable and deployable way to the target directory.

If you are using the command line, you can execute:

```
$ mvn package -DskipTests=true
```

This will create the executable and deployable WAR in the target directory. You can execute the WAR by running the following command:

```
$ java -jar target/rest-api-demo-0.0.1-SNAPSHOT.war
```

If you already have, for example, a Tomcat container, you can just drop the WAR file in the webapps/ folder and run your container. Try to rename the war when you are copying/moving it.

```
$ cp target/rest-api-demo-0.0.1-SNAPSHOT.war /opt/tomcat/webapps/rest-api-demo.war
$ /opt/tomcat/bin/startup.sh
```

Then you can open your browser and go to http://localhost:8080/rest-api-demo/currency/latest to get the same results.

More About Spring Boot

If you want to learn more about Spring Boot and its other useful features, I recommend my other book, *Pro Spring Boot* from Apress. It takes a more in-depth approach to this technology, from using the Spring Boot CLI through deploying it into the cloud.

Summary

This chapter introduced Spring Boot, discussed some of its features, and explained how it works with Spring MVC by creating a simple currency Restful application.

In the next chapter, you are going to start with the Spring Application events and listeners, which is a way to do messaging by emitting and consuming messages through the Observer pattern.

CHAPTER 3

■ ■ ■

Application Events

This chapter covers how to use the *observer pattern (behavioral pattern)* as a way to send messages to whoever needs them or whoever is listening. The chapter also shows how the Spring Framework implements this pattern through its application events, which can be declared as a simple interface implementation or by using specialized annotations.

The Observer Pattern

This particular pattern defines one-to-many dependencies between objects, so when one object (the subject) change its state, it needs to inform the others (observers) about this change. Then they can react to the change, as shown in Figure 3-1.

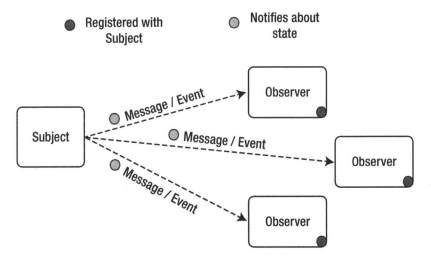

Figure 3-1. *The observer pattern*

There are many ways to implement this design pattern. The Java SDK includes the java.util. Observable class, which will set the change and notify the observers, as well as the java.util. Observer interface, which will receive the notification through its update method.

© Felipe Gutierrez 2017
F. Gutierrez, *Spring Boot Messaging*, DOI 10.1007/978-1-4842-1224-0_3

The Spring Framework has a sophisticated way to use this observer pattern and the recent versions (4.x) of Spring include even more improvements. They not only include this pattern but also have multiple events that allow you to determine more about the internals of the Spring container and to create your own events.

Remember that even though we are talking about the observer pattern and events, this is simply a way to communicate between components using messaging through events.

The Spring ApplicationEvent

You will find that the Spring Framework exposes the abstract org.springframework.context.ApplicationEvent class, which extends java.util.EventObject. The EventObject has an object where the event initially occurred. See Figure 3-2.

Figure 3-2. *The Spring ApplicationEvent hierarchy*

Figure 3-2 shows you the ApplicationEvent hierarchy, and as you can see, this class is extended by several events. It's worth mentioning at least two important events:

- ApplicationContextEvent (belongs to the Spring Framework):
  This is an abstract class where you have full access to the main central interface, which provides the entire configuration for your application. This class is also extended by the ContextClosed, ContextStartedEvent, ContextRefreshedEvent, and ContextStoppedEvent events to give you more details of the lifecycle of the Spring container.

- SpringApplicationEvent (belongs to Spring Boot): This is also an abstract class that contains all the information about the Spring Boot application through the SpringApplication class. The SpringApplication class is used to bootstrap and launch a Spring Boot application from a Java main method.

I chose these events because the project you are doing, the Rest API for currency exchanges, uses them. More about this later in this chapter.

Spring ApplicationListener

Now, for every event, you should have a way to receive the message. The Spring Framework has a main event listener. The `org.springframework.context.ApplicationListener` `<E extends ApplicationEvent>` interface extends from the `java.util.EventListener` (which is just a marker). The `ApplicationListener` is the main event listener for all the Spring `ApplicationContext` events, which you read about in the previous section. See Figure 3-3.

Figure 3-3. *ApplicationListener interface and hierarchy*

Figure 3-3 shows the ApplicationListener hierarchy and all the event listeners you can use. The Spring Framework will send the appropriate events on start, during runtime, and even upon normal shutdown in your Spring application. They will be filtered when the listener is invoked to match the event objects.

There are many use cases whereby you can use the ApplicationEvent or some of its implementations to listen (using the ApplicationListener) for incoming messages and then act on them. For example, in the Rest API currency project, discussed again in the next section, you determine when a user hits some of the Rest endpoints, and you then have a statistical way to see the traffic and recognize which endpoint is used more often.

Rest API Currency Project

Let's go back to the project and apply this type of design pattern to it. By implementing only the ApplicationListener of the ApplicationEvent type, the application will start listening for every event that happens during the Spring container initialization and part of the Beans lifecycle.

Take a look a Listing 3-1, which shows that the RestApiEventsListener class is a Spring component.

Listing 3-1. com.apress.messaging.listener.RestApiEventsListener.java

```
@Component
public class RestApiEventsListener implements ApplicationListener<ApplicationEvent>{

        public void onApplicationEvent(ApplicationEvent event) {

        }
}
```

Listing 3-1 shows you just part of the code where the RestApiEventsListener class implements the ApplicationListener of the ApplicationEvent event. You must implement the onApplicationEvent method that receives the ApplicationEvent as a parameter.

Again, one use case would be to determine how many times a Rest endpoint is being accessed. Look at Figure 3-2, where the ApplicationEvent hierarchy is—you will notice that there is a RequestHandledEvent and a ServletRequestHandledEvent that extends it. With the ServletRequestHandledEvent class, you can get the URL (endpoint) that is being accessed and create a counter for it. See Listing 3-2.

Listing 3-2. com.apress.messaging.listener.RestApiEventsListener.java

```
@Component
public class RestApiEventsListener implements ApplicationListener<ApplicationEvent>{

    private static final String LATEST = "/currency/latest";

    @Autowired
    private CounterService counterService;

    @Log(printParamsValues=true)
    public void onApplicationEvent(ApplicationEvent event) {
```

```
    if(event instanceof ServletRequestHandledEvent){
        if(((ServletRequestHandledEvent)event)
                    .getRequestUrl().equals(LATEST)){
            counterService
            .increment("url.currency.latest.hits");
            }
        }
    }
}
```

Listing 3-2 shows a little more of the code. Let's take a look at it:

- ServletRequestHandledEvent: This event is being published when there is a request to an endpoint. This is part of the web framework. This event contains all the web context information, which is why you can get the information about the URL being accessed.

- CounterService: This interface belongs to the spring-boot-actuator module, which allows you to have a metric by incrementing or decrementing a tag/property. In this case, the tag is url.currency.latest.hits.

- @Log(printParamsValues=true): This is a custom annotation that will be used as part of the before advice that logs all the information about the method being called. You can see the code in the com.apress.messaging. aop.CodeLogger.java class.

If you run the application, you will get some output generated from the @Log annotation (see Figure 3-4), but if you visit the /currency/latest endpoint a few times (see Figure 3-5), the application will start counting this endpoint as being accessed by using the CounterService instance. Then you can access this metric from the /metrics endpoint and see that the url. currency.latest.hits is being shown with the number of hits of that endpoint (see Figure 3-6).

```
2016-11-05 09:16:48.825  INFO 36482 --- [  restartedMain] o.s.b.a.e.mvc.EndpointHandlerMapping     : Mapped "{[/env/{name:.*}],methods=[GET],produces=[applica
2016-11-05 09:16:48.825  INFO 36482 --- [  restartedMain] o.s.b.a.e.mvc.EndpointHandlerMapping     : Mapped "{[/env || /env.json],methods=[GET],produces=[appl
2016-11-05 09:16:48.827  INFO 36482 --- [  restartedMain] o.s.b.a.e.mvc.EndpointHandlerMapping     : Mapped "{[/dump || /dump.json],methods=[GET],produces=[ap
2016-11-05 09:16:48.828  INFO 36482 --- [  restartedMain] o.s.b.a.e.mvc.EndpointHandlerMapping     : Mapped "{[/info || /info.json],methods=[GET],produces=[ap
2016-11-05 09:16:48.828  INFO 36482 --- [  restartedMain] o.s.b.a.e.mvc.EndpointHandlerMapping     : Mapped "{[/trace || /trace.json],methods=[GET],produces=[
2016-11-05 09:16:49.088  INFO 36482 --- [  restartedMain] o.s.b.d.a.OptionalLiveReloadServer       : LiveReload server is running on port 35729
2016-11-05 09:16:49.140  INFO 36482 --- [  restartedMain] o.s.j.e.a.AnnotationMBeanExporter        : Registering beans for JMX exposure on startup
2016-11-05 09:16:49.214  INFO 36482 --- [  restartedMain] o.s.c.support.DefaultLifecycleProcessor  : Starting beans in phase 0
2016-11-05 09:16:49.214  INFO 36482 --- [  restartedMain] com.apress.messaging.aop.CodeLogger      :
======================================
 Class: RestApiEventsListener
 Method: onApplicationEvent

 Param: ContextRefreshedEvent
 Value: org.springframework.context.event.ContextRefreshedEvent[source=org.springframework.boot.context.embedded.AnnotationConfigEmbeddedWebApplicationContext
======================================
2016-11-05 09:16:49.278  INFO 36482 --- [  restartedMain] s.b.c.e.t.TomcatEmbeddedServletContainer : Tomcat started on port(s): 8080 (http)
2016-11-05 09:16:49.280  INFO 36482 --- [  restartedMain] com.apress.messaging.aop.CodeLogger      :
======================================
 Class: RestApiEventsListener
 Method: onApplicationEvent

 Param: EmbeddedServletContainerInitializedEvent
 Value: org.springframework.boot.context.embedded.EmbeddedServletContainerInitializedEvent[source=org.springframework.boot.context.embedded.tomcat.TomcatEmbed
======================================
2016-11-05 09:16:49.323  INFO 36482 --- [  restartedMain] com.apress.messaging.aop.CodeLogger      :
======================================
 Class: RestApiEventsListener
 Method: onApplicationEvent

 Param: CurrencyEvent
 Value: com.apress.messaging.event.CurrencyEvent[source=com.apress.messaging.service.CurrencyService@118d3152]
--------------------------------------
```

Figure 3-4. *Console logs after running the rest-api-events project*

Figure 3-4 shows you some of the log output that you will see when running your application. These logs are the messages that the Spring Framework sends as ApplicationEvent events. Remember that this output is generated by the @Log annotation (a before AOP advice).

Figure 3-5 shows you some of the logs after accessing the /currency/latest endpoint a few times. You can see that the ApplicationEvent is an instance of the ServletRequestedEvent, which contains the requested URL.

```
2016-11-06 08:49:59.859  INFO 44519 --- [nio-8080-exec-7] com.apress.messaging.aop.CodeLogger      :
=================================
 Class: RestApiEventsListener
Method: onApplicationEvent

 Param: ServletRequestHandledEvent
 Value: ServletRequestHandledEvent: url=[/currency/latest]; client=[0:0:0:0:0:0:0:1]; method=[GET]; servlet=[dispatcherServlet]; session=[null]; user=[null]; time
=================================
2016-11-06 08:50:01.051  INFO 44519 --- [nio-8080-exec-8] com.apress.messaging.aop.CodeLogger      :
=================================
 Class: RestApiEventsListener
Method: onApplicationEvent

 Param: ServletRequestHandledEvent
 Value: ServletRequestHandledEvent: url=[/currency/latest]; client=[0:0:0:0:0:0:0:1]; method=[GET]; servlet=[dispatcherServlet]; session=[null]; user=[null]; time
=================================
```

Figure 3-5. *Console logs after visiting the /currency/latest endpoint*

Figure 3-6 shows you the /metrics endpoint (provided by the spring-boot-actuator dependency). At the bottom of the figure, you can see the "counter.url.currency.latest. hits":4 metric, which is updated by the CounterService instance (see Listing 3-2).

```
{
    mem: 608058,
    "mem.free": 186901,
    processors: 8,
    "instance.uptime": 78818,
    uptime: 85179,
    "systemload.average": 1.52197265625,
    "heap.committed": 527872,
    "heap.init": 262144,
    "heap.used": 340970,
    heap: 3728384,
    "nonheap.committed": 83200,
    "nonheap.init": 2496,
    "nonheap.used": 80186,
    nonheap: 0,
    "threads.peak": 37,
    "threads.daemon": 35,
    "threads.totalStarted": 48,
    threads: 37,
    classes: 10558,
    "classes.loaded": 10558,
    "classes.unloaded": 0,
    "gc.ps_scavenge.count": 10,
    "gc.ps_scavenge.time": 103,
    "gc.ps_marksweep.count": 2,
    "gc.ps_marksweep.time": 97,
    "httpsessions.max": -1,
    "httpsessions.active": 0,
    "datasource.primary.active": 0,
    "datasource.primary.usage": 0,
    "gauge.response.metrics": 16,
    "gauge.response.currency.latest": 5,
    "gauge.response.star-star": 2,
    "gauge.response.star-star.favicon.ico": 12,
    "counter.status.200.currency.latest": 4,
    "counter.status.200.star-star.favicon.ico": 1,
    "counter.status.200.metrics": 1,
    "counter.status.404.star-star": 3,
    "counter.url.currency.lastest.hits": 4
}
```


Figure 3-6. *http://localhost:8080/metrics*

Custom Events

So far, you have seen a way to create listeners for any `ApplicationEvent`, but what about when using custom events, ones that contain information about your domain object? This section shows you how to create a custom event.

To create a custom event, you must extend from `ApplicationEvent` so it's easy to publish it later.

Using the current project, imagine that you will send an event when there's an error (unchecked exception) during the call of any currency conversion. Maybe this will simply log the cause and show the object that caused the exception. Let's start by reviewing the `CurrencyConversionEvent` class, as shown in Listing 3-3.

Listing 3-3. com.apress.messaging.event.CurrencyConversionEvent.java

```java
package com.apress.messaging.event;

import org.springframework.context.ApplicationEvent;
import com.apress.messaging.domain.CurrencyConversion;

public class CurrencyConversionEvent extends ApplicationEvent {

    private static final long serialVersionUID = -4481493963350551884L;
    private CurrencyConversion conversion;
    private String message;

    public CurrencyConversionEvent(Object source, CurrencyConversion conversion) {
        super(source);
        this.conversion = conversion;
    }

    public CurrencyConversionEvent(Object source, String message, CurrencyConversion
    conversion) {
        super(source);
        this.message = message;
        this.conversion = conversion;
    }

    public CurrencyConversion getConversion(){
        return conversion;
    }

    public String getMessage(){
        return message;
    }
}
```

Listing 3-3 shows you a basic class that extends from ApplicationEvent and has two constructors. Each constructor will call its parent (ApplicationEvent) to set the source, set the current CurrencyConversion instance, and determine the message. In other words, you have the information needed to determine the source of errors in any currency conversion call.

Next, let's review the event listener that will receive the CurrencyConversionEvent. See Listing 3-4.

Listing 3-4. com.apress.messaging.listener.CurrencyConversionEventListener.java

```java
package com.apress.messaging.listener;

import org.slf4j.Logger;
import org.slf4j.LoggerFactory;
import org.springframework.context.ApplicationListener;
import org.springframework.stereotype.Component;
import com.apress.messaging.event.CurrencyConversionEvent;
```

```java
@Component
public class CurrencyConversionEventListener implements ApplicationListener<Currency
ConversionEvent> {

    private static final String DASH_LINE = "====================================";
    private static final String NEXT_LINE = "\n";
    private static final Logger log = LoggerFactory.getLogger(CurrencyConversionEvent
    Listener.class);

    @Override
    public void onApplicationEvent(CurrencyConversionEvent event) {
        Object obj = event.getSource();
        StringBuilder str = new StringBuilder(NEXT_LINE);
        str.append(DASH_LINE);
        str.append(NEXT_LINE);
        str.append("  Class: " + obj.getClass().getSimpleName());
        str.append(NEXT_LINE);
        str.append("Message: " + event.getMessage());
        str.append(NEXT_LINE);
        str.append("  Value: " + event.getConversion());
        str.append(NEXT_LINE);
        str.append(DASH_LINE);
        log.error(str.toString());
    }

}
```

Listing 3-4 shows you the listener that will receive all the CurrencyConversionEvent events. This class implements the ApplicationListener of type CurrencyConversionEvent, and it needs to implement the onApplicationEvent. As you can see, it is just logging the class, the message, and the CurrencyConversion domain object.

Next, let's see which class will be publishing the event when an error occurs. Let's review our CurrencyConversionService and the convertFromTo method, which has logic to get the currency codes. See Listing 3-5.

Listing 3-5. com.apress.messaging.service.CurrencyConversionService.java

```java
public CurrencyConversion convertFromTo(@ToUpper String base, @ToUpper String
code,Float amount) {
        Rate baseRate = new Rate(CurrencyExchange.BASE_CODE,1.0F,new Date());
        Rate codeRate = new Rate(CurrencyExchange.BASE_CODE,1.0F,new Date());

        if(!CurrencyExchange.BASE_CODE.equals(base))
                baseRate = repository.findByDateAndCode(new Date(), base);

        if(!CurrencyExchange.BASE_CODE.equals(code))
                codeRate = repository.findByDateAndCode(new Date(), code);
```

```
if(null == codeRate || null == baseRate)
        throw new BadCodeRuntimeException("Bad Code Base, unknown code:
        " + base, new CurrencyConversion(base,code,amount,-1F));

return new CurrencyConversion(base,code,amount,(codeRate.getRate()/baseRate.
getRate()) * amount);
}
```

Listing 3-5 shows you the convertFromTo method, which is doing the conversion by finding the rates based on the base and code variables. The if statement will throw a BadCodeRuntimeException, which has a constructor that accepts a string and a CurrencyConversion object. BadCodeRuntimeException is the unchecked exception that extends from RuntimeException (you can review that in the source code).

When the exception is thrown, we must publish the CurrencyConversionEvent and the error message, but adding this logic would mess up the code and soon we would have tangled, messy code. We can instead create an AOP that uses this exception when it's thrown. Listing 3-6 uses an AOP to publish the CurrencyConversionEvent event after throwing the exception.

Listing 3-6. com.apress.messaging.aop.CurrencyConversionAudit.java

```
@Aspect
@Component
public class CurrencyConversionAudit {

    private ApplicationEventPublisher publisher;

    @Autowired
    public CurrencyConversionAudit(
                    ApplicationEventPublisher publisher){
            this.publisher = publisher;
    }

    @Pointcut("execution(* com.apress.messaging.service.*Service.*(..))")
    public void exceptionPointcut() {}

    @AfterThrowing(pointcut="exceptionPointcut()",
                            throwing="ex")
    public void badCodeException(JoinPoint jp,
                            BadCodeRuntimeException ex){

        if(ex.getConversion()!=null){
            publisher.publishEvent(
                new CurrencyConversionEvent(
                            jp.getTarget(),
                            ex.getMessage(),
                            ex.getConversion()));
            }
        }

}
```

Listing 3-6 shows you @AfterThrowing, which knows about the BadCodeRuntimeException when it's thrown, and then executes the code inside the method. As you can see, it uses the ApplicationEventPublisher instance (which is being injected by the Spring Framework in the class constructor) and the publishEvent method, which sends the information about the class where the exception occurred, the message, and the CurrencyConversion object.

If you run the project and access /{amount}/{base}/to/{code} like this /1.0/usdx/to/mx, you will get something similar to Figure 3-7.

```
======================================
2016-11-06 18:24:24.004 ERROR 47845 --- [nio-8080-exec-1] c.a.m.l.CurrencyConversionEventListener  :
======================================
  Class: CurrencyConversionService
Message: Bad Code Base, unknown code: USDX
  Value: CurrencyConversion [base=USDX, code=MXN, amount=1.0, total=-1.0]
======================================
```

Figure 3-7. Log error in the CurrencyConversionService

As you can see, creating custom events is really easy. Remember these simple rules to use a custom event:

- Create an event class that extends from ApplicationEvent.

- Create an event listener class that implements the ApplicationListener of your custom event and implement the onApplication method.

- Use the ApplicationEventPublisher class to publish your custom event.

Using Event Listeners with Annotations

So far we have seen how to use and implement the ApplicationListener of type ApplicationEvent. This section shows you how to use some of the Spring-provided annotations as an easy way to listen for events.

@EventListener

The @EventListener annotation is a helpful annotation that you can use directly in the method that will handle the event. This means that there is no need to implement ApplicationListener anymore.

Listing 3-7 shows how you can use it.

Listing 3-7. com.apress.messaging.listener.RestAppListener.java

```
@Component
public class RestAppEventListener {

    @EventListener
    @Log(printParamsValues=true)
    public void restAppHandler(
            SpringApplicationEvent springApp){
        }
}
```

Listing 3-7 shows you the @EventListener annotation, which is applied to the restAppHandler method. The Spring Framework will wire everything up so this listener receives all the SpringApplicationEvent events. The SpringApplicationEvent is another event that extends from the ApplicationEvent abstract class but contains information about the Spring Boot application, like the arguments used in a command line, the banner, the resource loader, etc.

If you run the project, you will see something similar to Figure 3-8.

```
2016-11-06 20:43:28.676  INFO 48750 --- [ restartedMain] com.apress.messaging.aop.CodeLogger       :
===================================
 Class: RestAppEventListener
Method: restAppHandler

 Param: ApplicationReadyEvent
 Value: org.springframework.boot.context.event.ApplicationReadyEvent[source=org.springframework.boot.SpringApplication@14860744]
===================================
```

Figure 3-8. *Logs of the RestAppEventListener*

As you can see, the @EventListener annotation is simple to use. This annotation has even more features:

- It supports conditions, so it can be executed only if the expression given is true. For example:

  ```
  @EventListener(condition = "#springApp.args.length > 1")
  ```

  This snippet tells the listener to only use the events if the argument's length is greater than 1. If you replace the previous listener in Listing 3-7, you won't see the RestAppEventListener logs.

- You can listen for many events by passing an array of the event classes as the default value. For example:

  ```
  @EventListener({CurrencyEvent.class,
                  CurrencyConversionEvent.class})
  @Log(printParamsValues=true)
  public void restAppHandler(ApplicationEvent appEvent){ }
  ```

  This snippet listens for the CurrencyEvent and CurrencyConversion events in the same method, which now gets an ApplicationEvent instance. Also you can have no arguments and still listen for multiple events.

- When you have multiple events to listen to, you might want to prioritize them. You can add the @Order annotation to the method to do so. For example:

  ```
  @EventListener
  @Order(Ordered.HIGHEST_PRECEDENCE)
  @Log(printParamsValues=true)
  public void restAppHandler(SpringApplicationEvent springApp){
  }
  ```

  This snippet will be processed in the order of highest precedence.

- You can also process your event listeners in an asynchronous way, by adding the @Async annotation. For example:

```
@EventListener
@Async
@Log(printParamsValues=true)
public void restAppHandler(SpringApplicationEvent springApp){
}
```

@TransactionalEventListener

The Spring Framework 4.2.x and above versions introduce an additional annotation that allows you to listen for the transaction phase, such as a database transaction or any other transactions, including messaging events.

Let's start by using this annotation in the currency project. Look at the RateEventListener class shown in Listing 3-8.

Listing 3-8. com.apress.messaging.listener.RateEventListener.java

```
@Component
public class RateEventListener {

    @TransactionalEventListener
    @Log(printParamsValues=true,
            callMethodWithNoParamsToString="getRate")
    public void processEvent(CurrencyEvent event){ }
}
```

Listing 3-8 shows you the RateEventListener class, which uses the @TransactionalEventListener and processes the custom CurrencyEvent event (you can look at the code in the com.apress.messaging.event package). The @TransactionalEventListener will receive the events when a transactional channel is being established, either programmatically or by using the @Transactional annotation.

If you look at the com.apress.messaging.service.CurrencyService.java class, you will see the following code:

```
@Transactional
public void saveRate(Rate rate){
        repository.save(new
                Rate(rate.getCode(),
                    rate.getRate(),
                    rate.getDate()));
        publisher.publishEvent(new CurrencyEvent(this,rate));
}
```

This snippet shows the saveRate method, which is marked with the @Transactional annotation. It will publish a CurrencyEvent when it's done saving.

If you run the project you will see the logs about the RateEventListener several times. Take a peek at the main app (RestApiEventsApplication.java); you will see rates being saved using the CurrencyService instance and the logs of each transaction (after they are committed) by the RateEventListener listener. See Figure 3-9.

```
2016-11-06 21:12:07.511  INFO 48750 --- [ restartedMain] com.apress.messaging.aop.CodeLogger    :
===================================
 Class: RateEventListener
Method: processEvent

 Param: CurrencyEvent
 Value: Rate [code=EUR, rate=0.88857, date=2016-11-06]
```

Figure 3-9. *RateEventListener logs*

@TransactionalEventListener can listen for specific transaction phases. If you need to listen for events during a phase, you can use it like so:

```
@TransactionalEventListener(
      phase = TransactionPhase.BEFORE_COMMIT)
```

you can have: BEFORE_COMMIT, AFTER_COMMIT (default), AFTER_ROLLBACK and AFTER_COMPLETION.

■ **Note**   Remember that you can get all the code from the Apress site or directly from the GitHub Repository: http://www.apress.com/9781484212257

Summary

This chapter explained how the observer pattern works. It also covered the way the Spring Framework uses this pattern to expose application events.

It showed you some use cases whereby you can listen for application events and use them to count how many times an endpoint is being accessed by ServletRequestHandledEvent. It showed you how to create your own custom events by extending the ApplicationEvent abstract class.

You learned about an easy way to listen for events by using annotations such as the @EventListener. You also saw how to use the @TransactionalEventListener that is being triggered when a transaction happens, during, before, or after commit and after a rollback.

The next chapter covers the Java Message Service API and how you can do messaging using it.

CHAPTER 4

■ ■ ■

JMS with Spring Boot

The Java Message Service (JMS) was announced in June 2001 with version 1.0.2b. It's another solution for sending messaging between two or more clients. It was considered part of a Message Oriented Middleware (MOM) group of technologies at that time. The idea was to provide an API for a recurrent problem, a producer-consumer use case that allowed loosely coupled, reliable, and asynchronous components in a distributed environment.

This chapter starts with a simple project that will help you understand how the JMS clients work and how to configure it with Spring Boot. Then we are going to use this knowledge to build on the previous project, the currency REST API that now will be a receiver to save new rates. So, let's get started.

JMS

The JMS API provides two messaging models—*point-to-point* and *publish-subscribe*. Point-to-point is where messages are delivered to a receiver, and the delivery is guaranteed to only one consumer that is connected to a queue (see Figure 4-1).

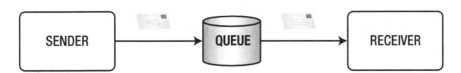

Figure 4-1. *The point-to-point messaging model*

The publish-subscribe model is where a message is delivered to zero or more consumers (normally called subscribers). The publisher creates a message topic for all the clients that want to subscribe to it (see Figure 4-2).

© Felipe Gutierrez 2017

F. Gutierrez, *Spring Boot Messaging*, DOI 10.1007/978-1-4842-1224-0_4

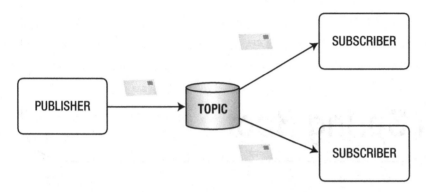

Figure 4-2. *The publish-subscribe messaging model*

JMS is a required API that needs to be implemented. In order to use or create JMS applications, you need to choose a *provider* (often called JMS server or broker) that will connect and decouple your senders/publishers from your receivers/subscribers, a *client* that will produce/send or receive/subscribe messages, a JMS *message* that contains the actual message (payload), and a JMS *queue* for a point-to-point messaging or a *topic* for a publish-subscriber scenario. We first talk more about the client.

JMS with Java

Let's first see how can you create a point-to-point sender client in Java; see Listing 4-1.

Listing 4-1. Point-to-Point Sender Client Snippet Code

```
//Step 1. Create the Connection
InitialContext ctx = new InitialContext();
QueueConnectionFactory factory = (QueueConnectionFactory)ctx.
lookup("connectionFactory");
QueueConnection connection = factory.createQueueConnection();
connection.start();

//Step 2. Create a Queue Session
QueueSession session = connection.createQueueSession(false, Session.AUTO_ACKNOWLEDGE);

//Step 3. Get the Queue object
Queue queue =( Queue)ctx.lookup("myQueue");

//Step 4. Create the Sender
QueueSender sender = session.createSender(queue);

//Step 5. Create the Message
TextMessage msg = session.createTextMessage();
msg.setText("Hello World");

//Step 6. Send the Message
sender.send(msg);
```

As you can see in Listing 4-1, this process is very straightforward. There are only six steps to send a text message. In Step 1, you need to know which connection process to use. Normally you need to include the jndi.properties file in your code with some information about your JMS provider; for example, if you use the Apache ActiveMQ, you need to specify its properties, as shown in Listing 4-2 (jndi.properties).

Listing 4-2. jndi.properties for Apache ActiveMQ

```
# Initial Context for the Apache ActiveMQ
java.naming.factory.initial=org.apache.activemq.jndi.ActiveMQInitialContextFactory

# This property must be the same as the one declared in the ctx.lookup statement.
# by default is: connectionFactory or ConnectionFactory
# connectionFactoryNames = connectionFactory, queueConnectionFactory,
queueConnectionFactory

#   Memory Broker = vm://localhost
# External Broker = tcp://hostname:61616
java.naming.provider.url=vm://localhost

# Queue naming rules:
# queue.[jndiName] = [physicalName]
queue.myQueue = apress.MyQueue

# Topic naming rules:
# topic.[jndiName] = [physicalName]
topic.myTopic = apress.MyTopic
```

Listing 4-2 shows the jndi.properties file that you need to include in every JMS application. In this case, it's using the Apache ActiveMQ settings and naming convention for the queues and topics.

Now, let's take a look at the receiver, shown in Listing 4-3.

Listing 4-3. Point-to-Point Receiver Client Snippet Code

```
// Step 1. Create Connection
InitialContext ctx = new InitialContext();
QueueConnectionFactory factory = (QueueConnectionFactory)ctx.lookup("connectionFactory");
QueueConnection connection = factory.createQueueConnection();
connection.start();

// Step 2. Create Session
QueueSession session = connection.createQueueSession(false, Session.AUTO_ACKNOWLEDGE);

// Step 3. Get the Queue
Queue queue=(Queue)ctx.lookup("myQueue");

// Step 4. Create the Receiver
QueueReceiver receiver = session.createReceiver(queue);
```

```java
// Step 5. Create the Listener
MessageListener listener = new MessageListener() {

                    @Override
                    public void onMessage(Message message) {
                        //Process the message here
                    }
            };

// Step 6. Register the Listener
receiver.setMessageListener(listener);
```

Listing 4-3 shows you the six steps needed to create a consumer for a point-to-point message. Of course, if you have this code in a separate project, you need to include `jndi.properties` as well (see Listing 4-2).

If you want to use the publisher-subscriber messaging model, you can create your publisher as shown in Listing 4-4.

Listing 4-4. Publisher-Subscriber Publisher Client

```java
//Step 1. Create the Connection
InitialContext ctx = new InitialContext();
TopicConnectionFactory factory =(TopicConnectionFactory)ctx.lookup("connectionFactory");
TopicConnection connection=f.createTopicConnection();
connection.start();

//Step 2. Create a Topic Session
TopicSession session = connection.createTopicSession(false, Session.AUTO_ACKNOWLEDGE);

//Step 3. Get the Topic object
Topic topic = (Topic)ctx.lookup("myTopic");

//Step 4. Create the Sender
TopicPublisher publisher = session.createPublisher(topic);

//Step 5. Create the Message
TextMessage msg = session.createTextMessage();
msg.setText("Hello World");

//Step 6. Send the Message
publisher.publish(msg);
```

Listing 4-4 shows you the publisher code—a publisher-subscriber message model—that will publish a simple text message to a topic named myTopic. Not too different from the point-to-point model. How about the subscriber? See Listing 4-5.

Listing 4-5. Publisher-Subscriber Subscriber Client

```
// Step 1. Create Connection
InitialContext ctx = new InitialContext();
TopicConnectionFactory factory = (TopicConnectionFactory)ctx.lookup("connectionFactory");
TopicConnection connection = factory.createTopicConnection();
connection.start();

// Step 2. Create Session
TopicSession session = connection.createTopicSession(false, Session.AUTO_ACKNOWLEDGE);

// Step 3. Get the Topic
Topic topic = (Topic)ctx.lookup("myTopic");

// Step 4. Create the Receiver
TopicSubscriber subscriber = session.createSubscriber(topic);

// Step 5. Create the Listener
MessageListener listener = new MessageListener() {

                @Override
                public void onMessage(Message message) {
                        //Process the message here
                }
        };

// Step 6. Register the Listener
subscriber.setMessageListener(listener);
```

Listing 4-5 shows the publisher-subscriber messaging client; this client subscribes to the topic named myTopic. You can run multiple clients with this code and each one will receive the message from the publisher; again not too different from the point-to-point model. Of course, you still need jndi.properties for these clients.

As you can see, both messaging model implementations are very straightforward. If you take a closer look to any of the code, you will notice that in every case, the message sent is just a text message, but what happens if you need to send something else? JMS supports different message types:

- StreamMessage is a serialized stream object.

- MapMessage consists of a name/value pairs, like a hash table.

- TextMessage is a string.

- ObjectMessage is a serializable object.

- ByteMessage is a raw stream of bytes.

As homework, try to create some clients (point-to-point or publisher-subscribe models) using these code snippets. The idea is to familiarize yourself on what you can do with this kind of messaging.

I've just given you a sneak peek on what you normally do with JMS without using an external framework. I think there are a lot of steps just to do something simple.

JMS with Spring Boot

Chapter 2 showed you how Spring Boot knows about the application you are trying to run because it's an opinionated technology. Just by adding a `spring-boot-starter` pom, you tell Spring Boot how to configure everything, right?

We are going to use Apache ActiveMQ in this example (you are welcome to use any other broker; the code will be the same), which means that we can include the `spring-boot-starter-activemq` dependency. By adding this dependency, Spring Boot will bring all the JMS and ActiveMQ (JAR files) that we will need for the applications and it will auto-configure all the necessary properties and extra configuration needed for the JMS client.

Remember all the steps that you needed to do in Java? These are not necessary with Spring Boot.

■ **Note**   We are going to use more dependencies like AOP to take care of some logging concerns. Take a look at the `pom.xml` file in the projects of these chapters.

We are going to work with the **jms-sender** project, which you can find in the book's source code. This project has a lot of the classes with some code commented out, and just by uncommenting, it should work. Don't worry, though, as I'll guide you through the following sections by explaining each snippet of code.

■ **Note**   Remember that you can get all the code from the Apress site or directly from the GitHub Repository at `http://www.apress.com/9781484212257`

Producer

Let's start by reviewing the producer using Spring Boot. Open the `com.apress.messaging.jms.SimpleSender.java` class. See Listing 4-6.

Listing 4-6. com.apress.messaging.jms.SimpleSender.java

```
@Component
public class SimpleSender {

    private JmsTemplate jmsTemplate;

    @Autowired
    public SimpleSender(JmsTemplate jmsTemplate){
        this.jmsTemplate = jmsTemplate;
    }
```

CHAPTER 4 ■ JMS WITH SPRING BOOT

```
    public void sendMessage(String destination,
                            String message){
        this.jmsTemplate.convertAndSend(destination, message);
    }
}
```

Listing 4-6 shows you the simplest and easiest way to create a producer. Let's analyze each part of the code:

- @Component: This annotation, as you probably already know, marks the class as a Spring bean, making it available at runtime.

- JmsTemplate: This is the most important piece of the client, because this class will send a message (among other things) to the JMS provider/broker.

- @Autowired: This annotation is used in the class constructor to inject the JmsTemplate bean (described before). You can even omit this annotation and Spring will figure out that you need this dependency here.

- convertAndSend: The JmsTemplate instance has this method and it converts the message. Because this is a string, it's converted automatically into a javax.jms.TextMessage and is sent to the destination, which is normally a queue.

Before you run this part of the code, let's examine the main application. Open the com.apress.messaging.JmsSenderApplication.java class, as shown in Listing 4-7.

Listing 4-7. com.apress.messaging.JmsSenderApplication.java

```
@SpringBootApplication
public class JmsSenderApplication {

    public static void main(String[] args) {
        SpringApplication.run(JmsSenderApplication.class, args);
    }

    @Bean
    CommandLineRunner simple(JMSProperties props,
                             SimpleSender sender){
        return args -> {
            sender.sendMessage(props.getQueue(), "Hello World");
        };
    }
}
```

Listing 4-7 shows you the main application. Let's consider each part:

- **@SpringBootApplication**: You already know this annotation. It's the way that Spring Boot identifying what type of application you are trying to run.

- **simple(JMSProperties,SimpleSender)**: This method is executed when the Spring container is ready to be used and will inject a **JMSProperties** and the **SimpleSender** beans for its use.

- **JMSProperties**: This class is used as a properties holder that reads the **application.properties** file and looks for the **apress.jms.queue** property (in this case set to **jms-sender**). If you want to know more, you can read more about it in the "Externalized Configuration" section in the Spring Boot reference.

Now you are ready to run this. (You can run it using the command line with Maven: $ **mvn spring-boot:run** or if you imported it into the STS, you can run it within the Boot Dashboard.) Once you run it, you will see something similar to Figure 4-3.

```
2016-11-16 20:14:39.036  INFO 31017 --- [ restartedMain] JMSAudit
=====================================
[BEFORE]
Method: sendMessage
Params:
> arg0: jms-demo
> arg1: Hello World
=====================================
```

Figure 4-3. *JmsSenderApplication logs*

Figure 4-3 shows you the logs once the application is running. The code is actually sending the message "Hello World" to the jms-demo queue. This means that you will see the JMSAudit text with some extra information. Where did I actually print this? Review the com.apress.messaging. aop.JMSAudit.java class. This class is an Around advice that is normally used for logging purposes. I know that for this example it's too much, but it gives me more ways to explore AOP.

You can see that this client is sending a message, but where is it? You know that we are using the spring-boot-starter-activemq dependency, but there doesn't seem to be any broker running. Where is it?

Remember that Spring Boot makes opinions based on your classpath dependencies, so by knowing that you have the spring-boot-starter-activemq dependency, it will see if you already have declared beans of type connectionFactory, session, sender, etc., so it can use them. If Spring Boot doesn't find anything, it will create all these by default and it will use the *in-memory* provider (the URL is vm://localhost). That's why there is no error at runtime and you can see that the message is sent.

Consumer

Next, let's look at the consumer. First I'll show you the consumer that uses the javax.jms. MessageListener interface (it's the same as before, in the JMS with Java section) to see what is needed to configure it. See Listing 4-8.

Listing 4-8. com.apress.messaging.jms.QueueListener.java

```java
@Component
public class QueueListener implements MessageListener {

    public void onMessage(Message message) {

    }
}
```

Listing 4-8 shows you the receiver that will listen for any messages in the queue (jms-demo). Let's review the code:

- @Component: If this is commented out, remove the // and add the right imports. I suggest you use the STS and press Cmd+Shift+O on a Mac or Ctrl+Shift+O on Windows. This annotation will mark the class as a Spring bean, so it can be used in the configuration.

- MessageListener: This interface is necessary to receive JMS messages, and it's necessary to implement the onMessage method.

- onMessage(Message): This is necessary to implement the method, and it has the actual message that is consumed from the queue.

As you can see, it's very simple, but if you try it to run it, you will see the same result as before. You'll see just the log about sending the message. Why is this? Well, you must tell Spring Boot how to use this listener, so take a look at Listing 4-9.

Listing 4-9. com.apress.messaging.config.JMSConfig.java

```java
@Configuration
@EnableConfigurationProperties(JMSProperties.class)
public class JMSConfig {

    @Bean
    public DefaultMessageListenerContainer
        customMessageListenerContainer(
                ConnectionFactory connectionFactory,
                    MessageListener queueListener,
            @Value("${apress.jms.queue}") final
                            String destinationName){
        DefaultMessageListenerContainer listener = new
                DefaultMessageListenerContainer();
        listener.setConnectionFactory(connectionFactory);
        listener.setDestinationName(destinationName);
        listener.setMessageListener(queueListener);
        return listener;
    }
}
```

Listing 4-9 shows you the configuration that you need to enable the QueueListener class. Let's review this class:

- **@Configuration**: This is a marker for the class to be taken as a Java config for the Spring container, so everything here will be used to set up Spring.

- **@EnableConfigurationProperties**: Remember that we were using the application.properties file to set the queue's name? This particular annotation will use the provided class (JMSProperties.class) as the property holder, so you can set some properties in the application. properties file. Later, you can get its value either by using @Value or by using the JMSProperties instance bean and the getters.

- **@Bean**: This is a marker to create a bean of type DefaultMessageListenerContainer in the Spring container.

- **DefaultMessageListenerContainer**: In this case, this is a return type that will be taken as a Spring bean. It has all the necessary information to determine the QueueListener class and what queue to consume from (destinationName).

- **ConnectionFactory**: Spring will inject this instance and it will auto-configure it using the defaults (unless you provide a custom ConnectionFactory). In this case, it will use the in-memory provider/broker.

- **MessageListener**: Spring will inject the QueueListener class (the receiver from Listing 4-8) so it can be used to set up the DefaultMessageListenerContainer instance.

- **@Value("${apress.jms.queue}")**: This annotation will inject the value "jms-demo" from the apress.jms.queue property that is in the application.properties file into the destinationName parameter.

Then, the actual method will create the DefaultMessageListenerContainer and set all its properties (connectionFactory, queueListener, and destinationName).

Now, if you run the application, you should get output similar to Figure 4-4.

```
2016-11-17 07:58:08.337  INFO 34103 --- [  restartedMain] JMSAudit                  :
=====================================
[BEFORE]
Method: sendMessage
Params:
> arg0: jms-demo
> arg1: Hello World
=====================================
2016-11-17 07:58:08.366  INFO 34103 --- [enerContainer-1] JMSAudit                  :
=====================================
[BEFORE]
Method: onMessage
Params:
> arg0: ActiveMQTextMessage {commandId = 5, responseRequired = true, messageId = ID:pivotal-es.local-64812-1479394688145-4:2:1:1:1, originalDestination = null,
=====================================
```

Figure 4-4. *Logs*

Figure 4-4 shows the onMessage method being called by consuming the message from the queue (remember that these logs are produced by the AOP aspect). If you take a closer look at the actual message, you should see something similar to this:

```
ActiveMQTextMessage {
    commandId = 5,
    responseRequired = true,
    messageId = ID:pivotal-es.local-64812,
    originalDestination = null,
    originalTransactionId = null,
    producerId = ID:pivotal-es.local-64812,
    destination = queue://jms-demo,
    transactionId = null,
    expiration = 0,
    timestamp = 1479394688357,
    arrival = 0,
    brokerInTime = 1479394688357,
    brokerOutTime = 1479394688362,
    correlationId = null,
    replyTo = null,
    persistent = true,
    type = null,
    priority = 4,
    groupID = null,
    groupSequence = 0,
    targetConsumerId = null,
    compressed = false,
    userID = null,
    content = null,
    marshalledProperties = null,
    dataStructure = null,
    redeliveryCounter = 0,
    size = 1046,
    properties = null,
    readOnlyProperties = true,
    readOnlyBody = true,
    droppable = false, j
    msXGroupFirstForConsumer = false,
    text = Hello World
}
```

As you can see, we are receiving an ActiveMQTextMessage that is an implementation around the javax.jms.TextMessage interface. It's important to know the destination property that points to the jms-demo queue, the payload, and the text property with its Hello World value.

You might wonder if there is a simpler way to configure the listener. How can you determine what to configure? Well, Spring Boot makes this even easier. You learn about this process in the next section.

Consumer with Annotations

The Spring Framework provides useful annotations for consuming messages, very similar to ApplicationEvents and Streams. Spring Boot helps auto-configure these annotations, thereby making it easier for the developer.

Let's first review the com.apress.messagin.jms.AnnotatedReceiver.java class. See Listing 4-10.

Listing 4-10. com.apress.messagin.jms.AnnotatedReceiver.java

```
@Component
public class AnnotatedReceiver {

    @JmsListener(destination = "${apress.jms.queue}")
    public void processMessage(String content) {

    }

}
```

Listing 4-10 shows you the AnnotatedReceiver class that includes the @JmsListener annotation:

- @Component: Remember, this is a marker for Spring to enable this bean in the Spring container.

- @JmsListener: This annotation is configured to create a message listener using the destination specified by the *SpEL* (Spring Expression Language) expression. In this case, it's the apress.jms.queue property that has the jms-demo value.

That's it! Spring Boot will configure everything for you, so no more beans to declare a message listener container.

■ **Note**   Before you run this receiver, first comment out the bean definition (DefaultMessageListenerContainer) in the JMSConfig class and the @Component in the QueueListener class.

It's now time to run this receiver (just remember to comment out the bean and listener, because you don't need them anymore). Once you run the application, you should have something similar to Figure 4-5.

```
2016-11-17 10:53:55.835  INFO 36359 --- [  restartedMain] JMSAudit
===================================
[BEFORE]
Method: sendMessage
Params:
> arg0: jms-demo
> arg1: Hello World
===================================
2016-11-17 10:53:55.870  INFO 36359 --- [enerContainer-1] JMSAudit
===================================
[BEFORE]
Method: processMessage
Params:
> arg0: Hello World
===================================
```

Figure 4-5. *@JmsListener logs*

Figure 4-5 shows you the logs after running the application. You can see that the method that's called is processMessage; this is the same message that was annotated by the @JmsListener annotation.

Currency Project

Let's talk about the currency project again. Imagine that you have a customer who wants to send a more accurate rate, but can only send rate messages using JMS. This means that your currency project needs to be a receiver, but the customer will need some kind of acknowledgement that you received the rate message.

Let's start by creating the sender client using the same jms-sender project. Review the com.apress.messaging.jms.RateSender.java class shown in Listing 4-11.

Listing 4-11. com.apress.messaging.jms.RateSender.java

```java
@Component
public class RateSender {

    private JmsTemplate jmsTemplate;

    @Autowired
    public RateSender(JmsTemplate jmsTemplate){
        this.jmsTemplate = jmsTemplate;
    }

    public void sendCurrency(String destination, Rate rate){
        this.jmsTemplate.convertAndSend(destination,rate);
    }
}
```

Listing 4-11 shows you the class you are going to use to send new Rate objects. As you can see, it's very similar to the SimpleSender class in Listing 4-6. The only difference is that instead of sending a text (String) message, it's now sending a Rate object. Take a look at the com.apress.messaging.domain.Rate.java class in Listing 4-12.

Listing 4-12. com.apress.messaging.domain.Rate.java

```
public class Rate {

    private String code;
    private Float rate;
    private Date date;

    public Rate() { }

    public Rate(String base, Float rate, Date date) {
        super();
        this.code = base;
        this.rate = rate;
        this.date = date;
    }

    //Setters and Getter omitted.

}
```

Listing 4-12 shows you the Rate domain class that you have already seen in the currency project, but remember that in previous chapter, we annotated it with @Entity and @Id as part of the JPA persistence. This time it will just be simple, because there is no need to persist the rate.

If you try to run the app at this point, you will get an error that says something like:

```
Cannot convert object of type [com.apress.messaging.domain.Rate] to JMS message.
Supported message payloads are: String, byte array, Map<String,?>, Serializable object.
```

We can implement Serializable into the Rate class, but the currency project doesn't have that. Now, if you remember, the idea was to create a REST API that accepts the JSON format, so let's see how can we use JSON here.

Open the com.apress.messaging.config.JMSConfig.java class. See Listing 4-13.

Listing 4-13. com.apress.messaging.config.JMSConfig.java

```
@Configuration
@EnableConfigurationProperties(JMSProperties.class)
public class JMSConfig {
```

```
@Bean
public MessageConverter jacksonJmsMessageConverter() {
    MappingJackson2MessageConverter converter = new
                MappingJackson2MessageConverter();
    converter.setTargetType(MessageType.TEXT);
    converter.setTypeIdPropertyName("_class_");
    return converter;
}
}
```

Listing 4-13 shows you the configuration needed to expose the message in the JSON format. Let's review it:

- MessageConverter: This is an interface that specifies a converter between Java objects and JMS messages. It exposes the toMessage and fromMessage methods. The Spring Boot auto-configuration will wire everything up to use this particular message converter.

- MappingJackson2MessageConverter: This class implements the MessageConverter interface and adds more methods to help with the conversion from/to JSON/object.

- setTargetType: This method is necessary to help the converter identify what type is needed to convert from/to. In this case, we are sending a JSON in a String format, which means that it will create a TextMessage object behind the scenes.

- setTypeIdPropertyName: This is an *important* setting, because it will drive the way the mapping is done behind the scenes. This can be any value you want. It's just a simple identifier that will hold the qualified class name that is being mapped.

That's enough to run the application again, but first let's see how the main app will look. See Listing 4-14.

Listing 4-14. com.apress.messaging.JmsSenderApplication.java

```
@SpringBootApplication
public class JmsSenderApplication {

    public static void main(String[] args) {
        SpringApplication.run(JmsSenderApplication.class, args);
    }

    @Bean
    CommandLineRunner process(JMSProperties props,
                                RateSender sender){
        return args -> {
                sender.sendCurrency(props.getRateQueue(),
                    new Rate("EUR",0.88857F,new Date()));
                sender.sendCurrency(props.getRateQueue(),
                    new Rate("JPY",102.17F,new Date()));
```

45

```
            sender.sendCurrency(props.getRateQueue(),
                 new Rate("MXN",19.232F,new Date()));
            sender.sendCurrency(props.getRateQueue(),
                 new Rate("GBP",0.75705F,new Date()));
        };
    }
}
```

Listing 4-14 shows you the main app (just remember to comment out the previous code). As you can see, it's very simple. We are just sending the new Rate objects. If you run the application, you should get the output shown in Figure 4-6.

```
2016-11-17 18:49:07.521  INFO 43138 --- [  restartedMain] JMSAudit
====================================
[BEFORE]|
Method: sendCurrency
Params:
> arg0: rates
> arg1: Rate [code=MXN, rate=19.232, date=2016-11-17]
====================================
```

Figure 4-6. *Logs when JMS sends a rate object*

Figure 4-6 shows you the logs without any errors. It's saying that everything went well and some rates were sent successfully. But this is not enough, because how can we guarantee that actually is a JSON format?

Using a Remote Apache ActiveMQ Broker

Let's use ActiveMQ as a remote broker. It will help us determine if the messages are actually going over to the broker instead of using the in-memory provider.

Make sure you have ActiveMQ up and running (you need to download it from http://activemq.apache.org/ and follow the installation instructions for your system). I used ActiveMQ version 5.14.0, but you can use any version. Before you run the application again, you need to make sure that it will be using the ActiveMQ broker that is running. Open the src/main/resources /application.properties file and uncomment out all the spring.activemq.* and the apress.jms.* properties. The result should look like Listing 4-15.

Listing 4-15. src/main/resources/application.properties

```
spring.activemq.broker-url=tcp://localhost:61616
spring.activemq.user=admin
spring.activemq.password=admin

#Apress Configuration
apress.jms.queue=jms-demo
apress.jms.rate-queue=rates
```

Listing 4-15 shows the `application.properties` file where the remote ActiveMQ is declared (in this case, it's the local system), the default port is `61616`, and the username and password are set to `admin`. With these properties in place, Spring Boot will configure the `connectionFactory` that will connect to the remote broker.

So, if you have the ActiveMQ broker running, you should be able to go to the `http://localhost:8161/admin` URL in your browser and see the web page shown in Figure 4-7.

Figure 4-7. *ActiveMQ web console: http://localhost:8161/admin*

Then you can execute the `jms-demo` application and select the queue from the web console to see that the queue called `rates` has been created (this name was based on the `apress.jms.rate-queue` property value). See Figure 4-8.

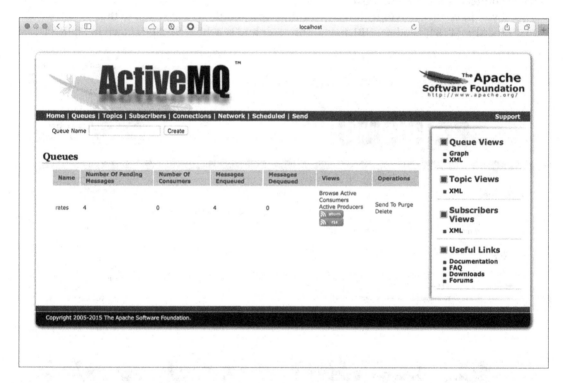

Figure 4-8. *ActiveMQ Queues tab*

If you click the queue called `rates`, you should see the four messages that were sent to the broker. See Figure 4-9.

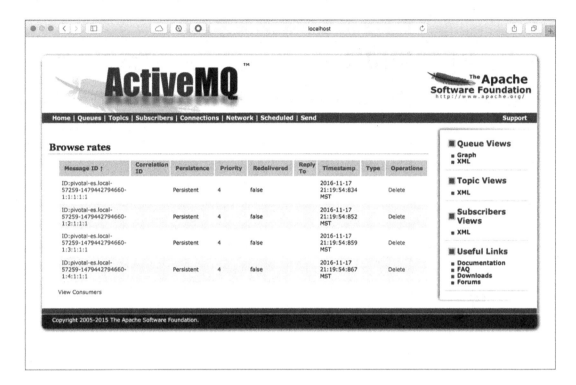

Figure 4-9. *ActiveMQ queue rate messages*

Click in any of the messages to see the content. See Figure 4-10.

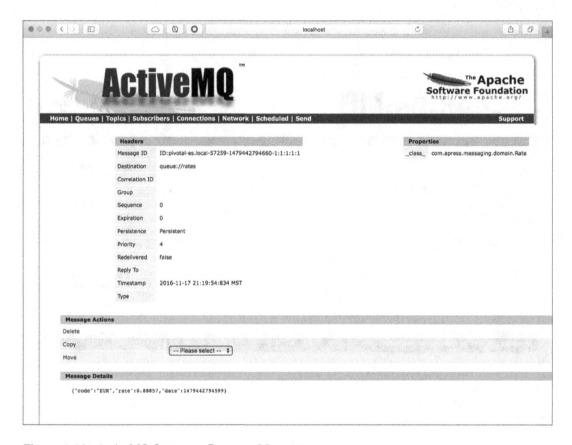

Figure 4-10. *ActiveMQ Queue --> Rates --> Message*

Figure 4-10 shows you the actual message received by the broker. Take a look at the message details; you will see something similar to this:

```
{"code":"EUR","rate":0.88857,"date":1479442794599}
```

The rate is sent by the jms-sender app. On the right, you can see a Properties legend where the
class property ID has the value of the com.apress.messaging.domain.Rate class (remember that this is important for the receiver as well, so it can convert back from JSON to object).

Now you know how to send objects that can be converted into JSON. Next, you need to receive this message, right? The sender needs to receive some acknowledgement from the receiver (it was part of the requirements) as well.

Reply-To

Spring JMS provides a way to reply to another queue, kind of like having a response-request/RPC model. You use it along with the listener, the @SendTo annotation.

In order to see this in action, we are going to work with the same jms-sender project. Remember to disable some of the components. You do this by commenting out the @Component annotations in all the listeners we have been working on.

Open the com.apress.message.jms.RateReplyReceiver.java class. See Listing 4-16.

Listing 4-16. com.apress.message.jms.RateReplyReceiver.java

```
@Component
public class RateReplyReceiver {

    @JmsListener(destination = "${apress.jms.rate-queue}")
    @SendTo("${apress.jms.rate-reply-queue}")
    public Message<String> processRate(Rate rate){
        //Process the Rate and return any significant value
        return MessageBuilder
                    .withPayload("PROCCESSED")
                    .setHeader("CODE", rate.getCode())
                    .setHeader("RATE", rate.getRate())
                    .setHeader("ID", UUID.randomUUID().toString())
                    .setHeader("DATE",
                            new SimpleDateFormat("yyyy-MM-dd")
                                    .format(new Date()))
                    .build();
    }

}
```

Listing 4-16 shows you the RateReplyReceiver.java class and the @SendTo annotation, which needs a value that will correspond to the reply-queue where the result message will be sent. Let's review it:

- @SendTo: This annotation will be the key to a reply. Make sure you still have the @JmsListener annotation, meaning that this method will act as a receiver and a sender. The method must have a return type. In this case, it will use the apress.jms.rate-reply-queue value to set the reply queue. The annotation value can be omitted if the main message has the JMSReplyTo header set.

- Message<T>: This is an interface that is built on the Generics type and provides useful getters, like getPayload and getHeaders. This is the preferred way to send a message.

- MessageBuilder: This is a helper class that allows you to enhance the message by allowing you to add more headers.

Next let's look again at the RateSender class. It not only will send the rate, but also will be listening to the reply-queue. Remember that the requirement was to receive some kind of acknowledgement from the receiver. See Listing 4-17.

Listing 4-17. com.apress.message.jms.RateSender.java

```
@Component
public class RateSender {

    private JmsTemplate jmsTemplate;

    @Autowired
    public RateSender(JmsTemplate jmsTemplate){
        this.jmsTemplate = jmsTemplate;
    }

    public void sendCurrency(String destination, Rate rate){
        this.jmsTemplate.convertAndSend(destination,rate);
    }

    @JmsListener(destination="${apress.jms.rate-reply-queue}")
    public void process(String body,@Header("CODE") String code){

    }
}
```

Listing 4-17 shows you the new RateSender class. As you can see, we are reusing the @JmsListener and and new @Header annotation. Let's review it:

- @JmsListener: You already know this annotation. The only difference is to include the correct name of the reply-queue. In this case, it's the apress.jms.rate-reply-queue property value.

- @Header: This annotation will provide you with direct access to the header of the Message<T>, and in this case it will be the rate code that was processed. Spring JMS has more options: @Headers brings a java.util.Map object, @Payload brings the actual payload, and @Valid turns on validation for your payload.

Before you run this, make sure you have the ActiveMQ broker up and running.

If you run the application you should have not only the sender, but also the receiver and the reply logs. See Figure 4-11.

```
2016-11-18 11:00:42.474  INFO 49565 --- [enerContainer-1] JMSAudit
=====================================
[BEFORE]
Method: processRate
Params:
> arg0: Rate [code=JPY, rate=102.17, date=2016-11-18]
=====================================
2016-11-18 11:00:42.478  INFO 49565 --- [enerContainer-1] JMSAudit
=====================================
[BEFORE]
Method: process
Params:
> arg0: PROCCESSED
> arg1: EUR
=====================================
```

Figure 4-11. *Logs with the reply-to queue*

You can take a look at the ActiveMQ web console and see that the reply-rate queue was created. See Figure 4-12.

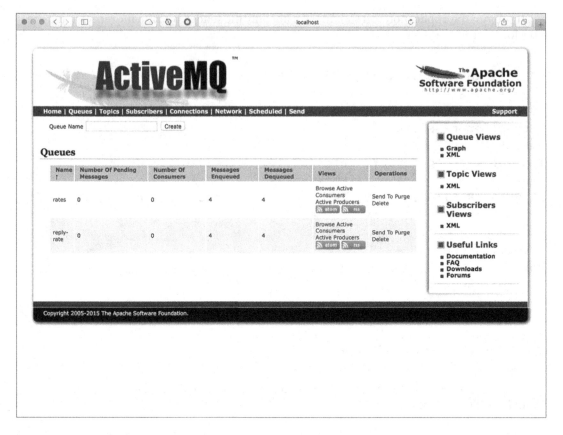

Figure 4-12. *Queues showing the reply-rate queue*

Now you know how to create a `reply-to` and have a kind of RPC mechanism for your applications.

Topics

This section discusses the next JMS messaging model, the publisher-subscriber or topics. This model has publishers that send messages to a topic and these topics can be from zero for multiple subscribers that will get a copy of the message. You need to think of this like a newspaper or a magazine subscription. You subscribe (to a particular interest—a topic) to receive a newspaper or magazine from the publisher.

This section continues with the `jms-sender` project, which will be the publisher. It also opens a new project within this chapter, the `jms-topic-subscriber` project. It's similar in structure to `jms-sender`.

In `jms-sender`, we are going to use the same `RateSender.java` and the main entry point where we send the rates, but there is one small change. Open the `src/main/resources/application.properties` file. It should look like Listing 4-18.

Listing 4-18. src/main/resources/application.properties

```
# Spring Web
spring.main.web-environment=false

#Default ActiveMQ properties
spring.activemq.broker-url=tcp://localhost:61616
spring.activemq.user=admin
spring.activemq.password=admin

#Apress Configuration
apress.jms.queue=jms-demo
apress.jms.rate-queue=rates
apress.jms.rate-reply-queue=reply-rate

#Enable Topic Messaging
spring.jms.pub-sub-domain=true

#Apress Topic Configuration
apress.jms.topic=rate-topic
```

Listing 4-18 shows the application.properties file, which has one particular property, the spring.jms.pub-sub-domain. This property by default is false, thereby making your producer send messages to a queue. When it's set to true, the producer (publisher) will send the message to a topic. This also applies to the listeners. If you set this property to true, the listeners will become subscribers of the topic.

Look at the last property as well. We are simply defining the name of the topic where all the subscribers will be listening.

You can now open and review the com.apress.messaging.jms.RateTopicReceiver.java class from the jms-topic-subscriber project and see that it's the same code (except for the name of the destination). In this project, you need to have the same application.properties file with the spring.jms.pub-sub-domain set to true (just make sure it has this property).

Now it's time to run the jms-topic-subscriber project. Before you run the jms-demo project, look at the Topics section of the ActiveMQ web console, as shown in Figure 4-13.

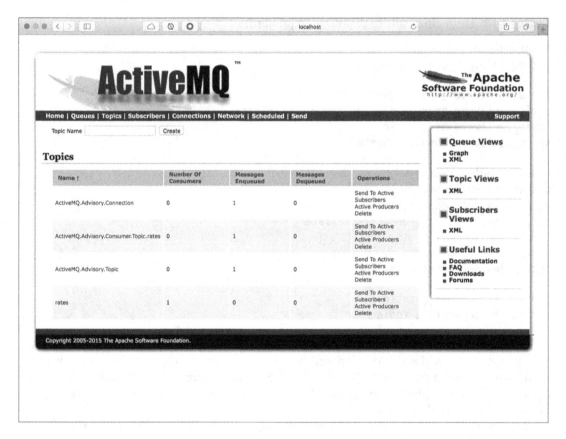

Figure 4-13. *The Topics section of the ActiveMQ web console*

Figure 4-13 shows that a topic called `rates` was created and there is a one consumer. Next, run the `jms-sender` project to see whether the rates are sent to the topic. Take a look at the `jms-topic-subscriber` project logs; you should see that you are consuming from the `rates` topic.

As an experiment, you can run multiple instances of the `jms-topic-subscriber` project (this is easy if you are using the STS and the Boot Dashboard) and verify that each one of them gets a copy of the rate. See Figure 4-14.

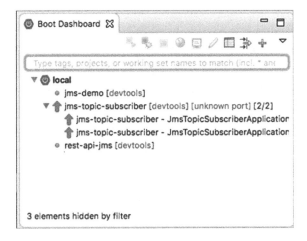

Figure 4-14. STS Boot Dashboard running two instances of the jms-topic-subscriber project

Currency Project

What do we need to do in order to use the currency project and start listening for new rates from other clients? The solution is already in the `rest-api-jms` project. This is what you need to do:

- Make sure you have the `application.properties`, `spring.activemq.*`, and `rate.jms.*` properties enabled.

- Review the `RateJmsReceiver` class and comment/uncomment out the listener you want to use (we have the simple listener and the listener with the `reply-to`).

- Review the `RateJmsConfiguration` class that has the JSON converter.

As homework, try to make it run. Remember that you will need to have the ActiveMQ broker up and running. Also, as an extra step, try to make this project topic-aware.

Summary

This chapter showed you how to use Spring Boot to send and receive messages using the JMS technology.

You saw the different JMS messaging models and what developers need to do to send or receive messages.

With Spring Boot, you saw how easy is to set up a JMS client and how, with simple annotation, you can have a functional application that uses JMS as a messaging system. Even though you just saw how to use Apache ActiveMQ as the broker, the same programming can be applied to HornetQ, IBM MQ, etc., just by providing the correct properties (connection factories and message listeners) in the `application.properties` file.

The next chapter discusses a different way to do messaging, using the Advance Messaging Queuing Protocol—AMQP.

CHAPTER 5

■ ■ ■

AMQP with Spring Boot

This chapter talks about the Advanced Messaging Queuing Protocol (AMQP), which is an agnostic message protocol. You'll learn how to use the Spring AMQP module, which will talk to a RabbitMQ broker. RabbitMQ is one of the most commonly used brokers around the globe and this is because it's easy to install and use. The best part is that it's open source.

AMQP comes from the financial sector and was created in 2003 by JPMorgan Chase. More companies then worked around it to enhance this new way to do messaging. Rabbit Technologies implemented AMQP with the Erlang programming language, and that's how RabbitMQ was born. Years later, VMware/Pivotal acquired it.

We are going to continue with some important definitions that will help you understand more about AMQP and RabbitMQ. This chapter uses the amqp-demo and rest-api-amqp projects. This chapter has all the code related to the amqp-demo and I'll let you dig into the rest-api-amqp project to complete the main requirement, which is to receive new rates from RabbitMQ and send them to interested consumers.

■ **Note** It's important to have the RabbitMQ server up and running for this chapter. You can download it from http://www.rabbitmq.com/download.html. Make sure you have at least the rabbitmq_management plugin installed, as it enables a web UI management for RabbitMQ. Once you have this set up, you can open your browser and point to http://localhost:15672 using guest as the username and password. More info about this web UI plugin can be found at http://www.rabbitmq.com/management.html.

The AMQP Model

This section covers the AMQP 0.9.1 model. Right now, this particular version is the most common.

The AMQP model is made up of messages that are published to *exchanges*. These *exchanges* distribute the messages to *queues* based on *bindings* (rules). The consumers then fetch/pull messages from these queues. See Figure 5-1.

© Felipe Gutierrez 2017   59
F. Gutierrez, *Spring Boot Messaging*, DOI 10.1007/978-1-4842-1224-0_5

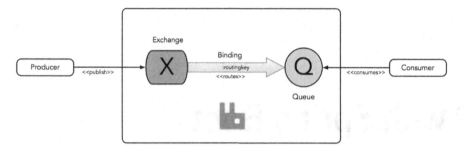

Figure 5-1. *The AMQP model*

You are going to see that normally as producer or consumer, you are required to create a *connection* to the broker and then use a *channel* (main transport) to publish a message to an exchange or consume a message from the queue. In other words, the AMQP protocol specifies multiplexed connections through channels.

The AMQP model has different features that allow the developer a lot of flexibility at the time of creating messaging applications. These features include message attributes (content-type, encoding, routing key, delivery mode, etc.), message acknowledgements, message rejection, message re-queue, multiplexed connection (channels), virtual hosts (to host isolated environments), multiple clients, and routing capabilities, among others.

Exchanges, Bindings, and Queues

These keywords are also known as AMQP entities. Let's define these entities (remember that all this is still part of the AMQP model):

- *Exchanges*: Entities where the producer sends messages. The exchange will use bindings to route the messages to the correct queue. The exchanges have the following properties: name, durability (can be durable or transient), auto-delete (the exchange is deleted when all the queues have finished using it), and arguments (hash map, broker dependent).

- *Bindings*: The rules that connect an exchange with another exchange or a queue. This is a string value.

- *Queue*: Store the messages (in memory or on disk) until they are consumed by applications. The queues have properties like name, durable (survive to a broker restart), exclusive (used by only one connection, which means the queue will be deleted when the connection is closed), auto-delete (the queue is deleted when the last consumer unsubscribes) and arguments (hash map, broker dependent).

The AMQP model provides four types of exchanges:

- *Direct exchange*: A one-to-one relationship with a queue through its binding. There is a default exchange that is a direct exchange type that uses the queue's name as a routing key for its binding.

- *Fanout exchange*: This exchange will copy a message for every queue bound to it. You must think as a broadcast; it's very similar to the publish/subscribe pattern (topic).

- *Topic exchange*: This exchange is similar to the direct exchange, the only difference being that it accepts wildcards (regex) for the routing keys by using the * (can substitute exactly one word) and # (can substitute zero or more words) options.

- *Headers exchange*: This exchange will do the routing by comparing multiple headers. You have to indicate if you want the headers to match exactly by adding the x-match:all (header: key) or match any of the headers by adding the x-match:any (header: key) to the same message header.

Figure 5-2 illustrates these exchange types.

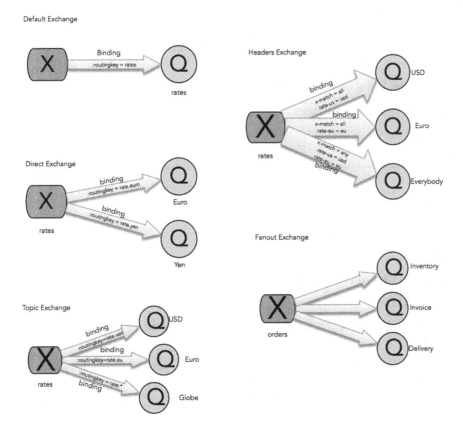

Figure 5-2. *Exchange types*

This little introduction is enough to get started with RabbitMQ and learn how to use it.

RabbitMQ

RabbitMQ is an open source broker that implements the AMQP model (from version 0.8.x to the 1.0 version of the AMQP model). RabbitMQ is written in the Erlang programming language, making it flexible and robust.

Here are some of its features:

- Distributed nodes
- Cluster ready
- Plugin based; the most important plugins are:
  - Federation
  - Shovel
  - Consistent hash
  - Community plugins
- Data/state replication with full ACID (Atomicity, Consistency, Isolation, Durability)
- Reliable and scalable out of the box: Federation and Shovel
- High availability with mirror queues
- Multi-protocol:
  - AMQP
  - MQTT
  - STOMP
  - SMTP
  - XMPP
- Web console and Rest API (for monitoring and administration)
- Secure: SSL and LDAP
- Multiple client libraries: Java, .NET, Ruby, Erlang, Python, Clojure, PHP, JavaScript, etc.

We could write an entire book defining every feature available, but what I want to do is give you a sense of what RabbitMQ can do. (If you need more info, you can get it at http://www.rabbitmq.com/features.html.) So, let's start using it by creating clients.

RabbitMQ with Spring Boot

Spring Boot relies on the Spring's spring-amqp project to do all the heavy lifting to connect, publish, consume, and manage the RabbitMQ broker. The spring-amqp project has been one of the most used modules in messaging application.

So, why do we need Spring Boot? Remember that Spring Boot is an opinionated runtime and it will help us configure what we need from the spring-amqp module by facilitating some properties that we can add to our application.properties file or by using a @Configuration class to override some of these opinions.

The spring-amqp project uses the known template pattern that exposes a RabbitTemplate class that allows us to publish and consume messages, among other tasks. It also provides easy-to-use message listeners that connect to the queues and consume messages. If you are worried about threading, transactions, reconnection (in case of failure), management, etc., you are covered with spring-amqp.

Producer

Let's start by using a simple producer. The ampq-demo project has everything you need to get started. Open the project and start with the simple producer shown in Listing 5-1.

Listing 5-1. com.apress.messaging.amqp.Producer

```
@Component
public class Producer {

        private RabbitTemplate template;

        @Autowired
        public Producer(RabbitTemplate template){
                this.template = template;
        }

    public void sendMessage(String exchange,
                        String routingKey, String message){
        this.template.convertAndSend(exchange,
                                routingKey, message);
    }
}
```

Listing 5-1 shows a simple amqp producer. Let's analyze the important parts of the code:

- @Component: This is a marker from the Spring framework that will recognize this class as a Spring Bean so you can use it in the application. You will see this in action in the main application next.

- RabbitTemplate: This is one of the main classes from the Spring AMQP module that brings a lot of functionality to interact with RabbitMQ, like send, receive, and do admin tasks in RabbitMQ. In this example, it's used to convert and send a message to the broker. Remember that, in order to interact with RabbitMQ, you must open a connection and create a channel (from that connection) and then send the message to the exchange. This setup will be handled by the RabbitTemplate instance.

- convertAndSend: This method will convert the message to the right type (into a byte array) and will send it to the RabbitMQ broker. This particular method has three parameters. The first one is the name of the exchange (where the message will be sent through the channel), the second parameter is the routing key (the binding rule that will route the message to the right queue), and the message, which in this case is just a string.

As you can see, this is a very simple producer. It's worth mentioning that the RabbitTemplate class has a variety of overload methods that help you send, listen, use custom converters, and do specialized tasks (you will read more about this later).

Next, let's see how can we use this producer. Open the AmqpDemoApplication.java class shown in Listing 5-2.

Listing 5-2. com.apress.messaging.AmqpDemoApplication.java

```java
@SpringBootApplication
public class AmqpDemoApplication {

    public static void main(String[] args) {
        SpringApplication.run(AmqpDemoApplication.class, args);
    }

    @Bean
        CommandLineRunner simple(
        @Value("${apress.amqp.exchange:}")String exchange,
        @Value("${apress.amqp.queue}")String routingKey,
                                        Producer producer){
        return args -> {
                    producer.sendMessage(
                        exchange,
                        routingKey, "HELLO AMQP!");
        };
    }
}
```

Listing 5-2 shows you the main Spring Boot application. Let's review the code:

- @Bean CommandLineRunner: You are already familiar with this annotation and interface. It will be executed when the Spring container has initialized all the beans and is ready to be used.

- @Value("${apress.amqp.exchange:}"): This annotation evaluates the properties (through application.properties, command-line arguments, or environment variables) that include the apress.amqp.exchange key. If it's not found, it will use just an empty string, which is the : after the exchange.

- @Value("${apress.amqp.queue}"): This annotation will evaluate the properties (through the application.properties, command-line arguments, or environment variables) that include the apress.amqp. queue key. This key is mandatory, so you will find it in the src/resources/ application.properties file with the spring-boot-queue value.

- Producer: This is the simple producer class (shown in Listing 5-1). As you can see, we are using the sendMessage method to send the exchange's name, the routing key, and the "HELLO AMQP!" message.

Before you test it, you need to make sure that your RabbitMQ broker is up and running. You also have to set up your exchange, binding, and the queue, although you don't need to do this here because the amqp-demo project already has this configuration set up this for you. Take a look at the AMQPConfig.java class shown in Listing 5-3.

Listing 5-3. com.apress.messaging.config.AMQPConfig.java

```java
@Configuration
@EnableConfigurationProperties(AMQPProperties.class)
public class AMQPConfig {
    @Bean
    public Queue queue(
            @Value("${apress.amqp.queue}")String queueName){
        return new Queue(queueName,false);
    }
}
```

Listing 5-3 shows you the AMQPConfig that defines the following:

- @EnableConfigurationProperties: This will declare a custom properties that will have the prefix: apress.amqp.*. That's why we can use the apress. amqp.queue or apress.amqp.exchange keys.

- @Bean Queue: This is the important part where programmatically we are declaring the queue that (in this case) will be created by returning a new instance of the Queue class.

- @Value("${apress.amqp.queue}"): This annotation will evaluate the key apress.amqp.queue that is defined in the src/main/resources/ application.properties that has the spring-boot-queue value.

I think this configuration is very straightforward, but if you think about it, it looks like we are missing the Exchange declaration and the binding that routes to the queue. Well, every time you create a queue in RabbitMQ, it's bound to a *default exchange* (normally just declared as an empty string) and the routing key happens to be the name of the queue. As you can see, we are passing the name of the queue as the routing key to the producer instance.

You can now run the application and see in the RabbitMQ Management Console that the spring-boot-queue was created and has one message. The output is shown in Figure 5-3.

```
2016-12-10 20:04:22.849  INFO 45508 --- [  restartedMain] AMQPAudit
====================================
[BEFORE]
Method: sendMessage
Params:
> arg0:
> arg1: spring-boot-queue
> arg2: HELLO AMQP!

[AFTER]
Return: void/null
====================================
```

Figure 5-3. *Producer logs*

Figure 5-3 shows you the logs. In the amqp-demo project, you will find the com.apress. messaging.aop.AMQPAudit.java class. It's an Around advice that will log the Producer method call. See Figure 5-4.

Figure 5-4. *RabbitMQ Management Console (http://localhost:15672/#/queues): spring-boot-queue*

Figure 5-4 shows you the RabbitMQ Management Console, where you can see that the queue was created and the message was sent.

Do you know how are we connecting to the RabbitMQ broker? What happens if I have a remote server and I need to specify where to connect, passing an IP or maybe a username or password?

Spring Boot will figure this out, because Spring Boot is an opinionated runtime and it will find the `spring-boot-starter-amqp` dependencies in the classpath and will ask if you already have a `ConnectionFactory` (that will connect to the RabbitMQ) with all the necessary information about the broker. If you do not, it will attempt to use the default settings and look for the local broker.

If you want to specify a remote broker, you do so by providing the `spring.rabbitmq.*` properties in the `src/main/resources/application.properties` file. This is enough to connect to a remote RabbitMQ.

Consumer

Now, let's talk about how we consume the message that we sent using the producer. Open the `Consumer.java` class shown in Listing 5-4

Listing 5-4. com.apress.messaging.amqp.Consumer.java

```
@Component
public class Consumer implements MessageListener{

        public void onMessage(Message message) {

        }
}
```

Listing 5-4 shows you the simplest consumer code. This is an asynchronous consumer that implements a `org.springframework.amqp.core.MessageListener` interface and the `onMessage` method. This method will receive the message as an `org.springframework.amqp.core.Message` instance. In order to use this consumer, you need to provide Spring Boot with some useful configuration settings. Open the `AMQPConfig` java class. See Listing 5-5.

Listing 5-5. com.apress.messaging.config.AMQPConfig.java

```
@Configuration
@EnableConfigurationProperties(AMQPProperties.class)
public class AMQPConfig {
    @Bean
    public Queue queue(
            @Value("${apress.amqp.queue}")String queueName){
                return new Queue(queueName,false);
    }
```

```
@Bean
public SimpleMessageListenerContainer
            container(ConnectionFactory connectionFactory,
                      MessageListener consumer,
        @Value("${apress.amqp.queue}")String queueName) {

    SimpleMessageListenerContainer container = new
                        SimpleMessageListenerContainer();
        container.setConnectionFactory(connectionFactory);
        container.setQueueNames(queueName);
        container.setMessageListener(consumer);
        return container;
    }
}
```

Listing 5-5 shows you the augmented AMQPConfig class (from listing 5-3), where we have the following:

- SimpleMessageListenerContainer: This class creates a message listener container that will listen to the queue for any messages. This class needs to be set up with a connection factory, a message listener handler, and the name of the queue(s). As you can see, this is a bean that we need to return to initiate the message listener container.

- ConnectionFactory: This interface is mandatory for the SimpleMessage ListenerContainer class, because it's the one that knows about the RabbitMQ broker (host, username, password, vhost, etc.). It's important to know that this connection factory is being wired up by Spring Boot, either by using the default settings (no configuration at all) or by specifying its properties in the application.properties file with the spring.rabbitmq.* properties. You can also declare your own ConnectionFactory as a bean (by declaring the @Bean in a method).

- MessageListener: As you can see, this is one of the parameters of the method container (consumer), and Spring will register the com.apress. messaging.amqp.Consumer class as a handler. It's then used when calling the container.setMessageListener method.

Note that we are using the queueName, which is being wired up by Spring Boot by using the apress.amqp.queue property.

That's pretty much it. You now have a complete producer and consumer. You can run the program and see the logs shown in Figure 5-5.

```
===================================
2016-12-10 20:30:39.381  INFO 47446 --- [      container-1] AMQPAudit
===================================
[BEFORE]
Method: onMessage
Params:
> arg0: (Body:'HELLO AMQP!' MessageProperties [headers={}, timestamp=null,

[AFTER]
Return: void/null
===================================
```

Figure 5-5. *Consumer logs*

Figure 5-5 shows you the logs of the consumer. Note that the method that's called is onMessage and it's represented by the org.springframework.amqp.core.Message instance.

Consumer Using Annotations

Wait a minute! I told you Spring Boot does this easier, right? In the current example, we needed to register our container and implement the MessageListener interface. The good thing is that the Spring AMQP provides a way to use annotations and, with the help of Spring Boot, everything is configured the right way.

Go to your AMQPConfig class and remove the container method. It should look like Listing 5-3. Open the com.apress.messaging.amqp.AnnotatedConsumer class; it should look like Listing 5-6.

Listing 5-6. com.apress.messaging.amqp.AnnotatedConsumer.java

```java
@Component
public class AnnotatedConsumer {

        @RabbitListener(queues="${apress.amqp.queue}")
        public void process(String message){

        }
}
```

Listing 5-6 shows you how to create a consumer without creating a container, simply by adding the @RabbitListener annotation. Spring AMQP will create the container for you, and it will wire everything up with Spring Boot's help. As you can see, it uses queues as the parameter and it's using the apress.amqp.queue property. See also that the method receives a String (and not a Message object). You can use your own object, which would require an extra step. Don't worry, as we are going to do this in later sections.

You can now run the project and you should get something similar to Figure 5-6.

```
2016-12-30 21:32:09.661  INFO 5487 --- [cTaskExecutor-1] AMQPAudit
====================================
[BEFORE]
Method: process
Params:
> arg0: HELLO AMQP!

[AFTER]
Return: void/null
====================================
```

Figure 5-6. *Consumer with the @RabbitListener annotation*

As you can see, it's very simple to create a producer and consumer with just a few lines of code. Next, let's review how can we create and use an RPC model.

RPC

The Remote Procedure Call (RPC) model was one of the many use cases back in the 60s, when distributed computing was a challenge (it *still* is). The RPC model is considered a request-response protocol, where you have a client that starts a process by sending a request message to a remote server to execute one or several tasks. Then the remote server sends a response to the client so it can continue with the process. See Figure 5-7.

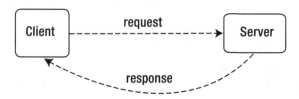

Figure 5-7. *Simple RPC model*

Creating an RPC messaging model in Spring Boot is very easy. Remember that Spring Boot relies on the Spring AMQP module so you don't have to configure the RabbitMQ broker. The Spring AMQP will take care of that. Let's review the code so you get a better picture of what's going on.

Open the `com.apress.messaging.amqp.RpcClient` class. It should look like Listing 5-7.

Listing 5-7. com.apress.messaging.amqp.RpcClient.java

```
@Component
public class RpcClient {

    private RabbitTemplate template;

    @Autowired
    public RpcClient(RabbitTemplate template) {
        this.template = template;
    }

    public Object sendMessage(String exchange,
                    String routingKey, String message) {
        Object response =
                this.template
                        .convertSendAndReceive(exchange, routingKey, message);
        return response;
    }
}
```

Listing 5-7 shows you the RpcClient class, and if you compare it to Listing 5-1 (the Producer class), you will notice that there is only one difference—the template method being called. In this example, we are using the convertSendAndReceive method, which accepts three parameters—an exchange name, the routing key, and the message. It returns an object (the return will normally be wrapped into it as an org.springframework.amqp.core.Message instance). Of course, you can find more overloaded methods from this signature, but for now, we are going to make it as simple as possible.

Next, let's take a look at the server. Open the com.apress.messaging.amqp.RpcServer class. See Listing 5-8.

Listing 5-8. com.apress.messaging.amqp.RpcServer.java

```
@Component
public class RpcServer {

    @RabbitListener(queues="${apress.amqp.queue}")
        public Message<String> process(String message){

        //More Processing here...

        return MessageBuilder
                .withPayload("PROCESSED:OK")
                .setHeader("PROCESSED", new
                                SimpleDateFormat("yyyy-MM-dd")
                                                .format(new Date()))
                .setHeader("CODE", UUID.randomUUID().toString())
                .build();
    }
}
```

71

Listing 5-8 shows you the RpcServer class. Let's see what is new and different from the other versions:

- @RabbitListener: You are already familiar with this annotation. It will create a message listener container and it will be listening for any incoming messages from the apress.amqp.queue queue (remember that this is a property specified in the application.properties file).

- Message<String>: If you want to enhance your message, this is what you need to return, because it gives you a way to use headers. In this example, we are using a string type message.

- MessageBuilder: This is a helper class that allows you to build a new message, add/copy headers, and more. As you can see, we are just creating a new message with a payload set to PROCESSED:OK and adding several headers.

If you take a closer look at Listing 5-8, you will notice that the process method handler returns a Message of type String, and because of that, the Spring AMQP uses the RabbitMQ's direct reply-to feature. That feature allows us to connect the server to the client for a response without creating a reply-queue (this has been a feature since version 3.4.x of the RabbitMQ broker).

You don't need to worry about any correlation data, because Spring AMQP will create it for you. You also have a way to customize it or create your own correlation data.

Now, let's take a look at the main application. Open your com.apress.messaging. AmqpDemoApplication class; it should look like Listing 5-9.

Listing 5-9. com.apress.messaging.AmqpDemoApplication.java

```java
@SpringBootApplication
public class AmqpDemoApplication {

    public static void main(String[] args) {
        SpringApplication.run(AmqpDemoApplication.class, args);
    }

    @Bean
    CommandLineRunner
    simple(@Value("${apress.amqp.exchange:}")String exchange,
            @Value("${apress.amqp.queue}")String routingKey,
            RpcClient client){
                return args -> {
                    Object result = client
                            .sendMessage(exchange,
                                        routingKey,
                                    "HELLO AMQP/RPC!");
                    assert result!=null;
            };
    }
}
```

Listing 5-9 shows the main app where you are only using the RpcClient.

Before you run the RPC example, make sure you don't have another listener using the same queue.

By running the app, you should get something similar to Figure 5-8.

```
2017-01-02 11:17:39.239  INFO 88079 --- [cTaskExecutor-1] AMQPAudit                          :
====================================
[BEFORE]
 Class: com.apress.messaging.amqp.RpcServer
Method: process
Params:
> arg0: HELLO AMQP/RPC!

[AFTER]
Return: GenericMessage [payload=PROCESSED:OK, headers={PROCESSED=2017-01-02, CODE=83381921-1ad1-4c8a-8f95-840d4733fc1c,
====================================
2017-01-02 11:17:39.240  INFO 88079 --- [  restartedMain] AMQPAudit                          :
====================================
[BEFORE]
 Class: com.apress.messaging.amqp.RpcClient
Method: sendMessage
Params:
> arg0:
> arg1: spring-boot-queue
> arg2: HELLO AMQP/RPC!

[AFTER]
Return: PROCESSED:OK
====================================
```

Figure 5-8. *RPC model logs*

Sometimes you will need to have more control over the RPC. Maybe you want to have a fixed queue that is used to do the reply, for example. For that, you need to add some configuration to the application. See Listing 5-10.

Listing 5-10. com.apress.messaging.config.AMQPConfig.java

```
@Configuration
@EnableConfigurationProperties(AMQPProperties.class)
public class AMQPConfig {

@Configuration
@EnableConfigurationProperties(AMQPProperties.class)
public class AMQPConfig {

    @Autowired
    ConnectionFactory connectionFactory;

    @Value("${apress.amqp.reply-queue}")
    String replyQueueName;
```

```
@Bean
public RabbitTemplate fixedReplyQueueRabbitTemplate() {
    RabbitTemplate template = new
                RabbitTemplate(connectionFactory);
            template.setReplyAddress(replyQueueName);
            template.setReplyTimeout(60000L);
            return template;
}

@Bean
public SimpleMessageListenerContainer
                    replyListenerContainer() {

    SimpleMessageListenerContainer container = new
                SimpleMessageListenerContainer();

    container.setConnectionFactory(connectionFactory);
     container.setQueues(replyQueue());
     container.setMessageListener(
                fixedReplyQueueRabbitTemplate());
        return container;
}

@Bean
public Queue replyQueue(){
    return new Queue(replyQueueName,false);
}

@Bean
    public Queue queue(
        @Value("${apress.amqp.queue}")String queueName){
            return new Queue(queueName,false);
    }
}
```

Listing 5-10 shows you how to set up a fixed queue that will be used by the server to reply to the client request, and the client will be listening to. The important part here is the RabbitTemplate, which will configure the reply-to queue by using the setReplyAddress method. It's also necessary to use the same template as the listener in order to listen for responses from the server (this is accomplished by setting the listener container to setMessageListener).

■ **Note** The RabbitMQ Java client (https://www.rabbitmq.com/java-client.html) provides out-of-the-box RPC client/server classes, but you still need to deal with reconnections, transactions, etc., which is something that Spring AMQP does for you.

Reply Management

One of the cool things about using Spring AMQP is that it has some really nice features. For example, you can create an actual reply-to scenario using an exchange and a routing key. In other words, you send a message without waiting for a response (kind of a fire and forget) and you reply to a specific exchange/queue that will have another flow.

Spring AMQP includes the @SendTo annotation, whereby you can send your reply to an exchange or to a queue. Open the com.apress.messaging.amqp.ReplyToService class shown in Listing 5-11.

Listing 5-11. com.apress.messaging.amqp.ReplyToService.java

```
@Component
public class ReplyToService {

    @RabbitListener(queues="${apress.amqp.queue}")
    @SendTo("${apress.amqp.reply-exchange-queue}")
    public Message<String> replyToProcess(String message){

        //More Processing here...

        return MessageBuilder
                .withPayload("PROCESSED:OK")
                .setHeader("PROCESSED", new
                        SimpleDateFormat("yyyy-MM-dd")
                            .format(new Date()))
                .setHeader("CODE", UUID.randomUUID().toString())
                .build();
    }

}
```

Listing 5-11 shows the @SendTo annotation. As you can see, the replyToProcess method is also annotated with @RabbitListener. This means that it will be listening to a queue (provided by the apress.amqp.queue property value). The important part here is that it will return a message that will be sent to the exchange/routing-key (provided by the apress.amqp.reply-exchange-queue property value) as a reply-to mechanism by the @SendTo annotation.

You can use the Producer class to send the message (see Listing 5-2), but before you run this example, you need to do the following using the RabbitMQ Web Console:

- Create a direct exchange called my-exchange

- Create a queue (using any name you want)

- Bind my-exchange to the queue you just created using the my-reply-rk routing key

Of course, you can also create this programmatically (may be as homework?).

Now you are ready to experiment with this. Run the example and you should have a message in the queue you have created. As you can see, you have another way to do reply-to and create another flow.

Flow Control

Flow control is one of the best features of RabbitMQ. It will reduce the speed of connections of the publishers that are sending messages that can't be consumed fast enough.

RabbitMQ will normally reduce the speed and sometimes it will block the connections, preventing them from flooding. It's good to know about this feature because you can use it to determine where your bottleneck is. Either you increase the number of concurrent consumers to the queue or you review the customer's code to determine why it's taking too long to process a message.

So, how easy is it to find these bottlenecks? One way to find them is to monitor your RabbitMQ console and see if you are triggering the flow control mechanism. You can determine this by checking the status of the Connections or Channels tabs, They are normally yellow and say "Flow Control". However, there is an easier way. RabbitMQ send events that allow you to react to flow control and complete a shutdown.

Blocking/Unblocking Events

Spring AMQP provides a mechanism for attaching the Block, Unblock, and the Shutdown events. You can find the code in the com.apress.messaging.config.AMQConfig class.

If you want to listen for the Block or Unblock events, just add the following code to your configuration, the BlockedListener event:

```
@Bean
public RabbitTemplate rabbitTemplate(ConnectionFactory
                                        connectionFactory){
        RabbitTemplate template = new
                    RabbitTemplate(connectionFactory);
        template.execute(new ChannelCallback<Object>() {

            public Object
            doInRabbit(Channel channel) throws Exception {

                channel.getConnection().addBlockedListener(
                        new BlockedListener() {

                        public void handleUnblocked()
                                throws IOException{
                            // Resume business logic
                        }

                        public void handleBlocked(String reason)
                                throws IOException {
                            // FlowControl -> Logic to handle block
                        }
            });
```

```
                    return null;
            }

        });
    return template;
}
```

If you only want to listen for a failure or a Rabbit shutdown, you can use the following code, the ShutdownListener event:

```
@Bean
public RabbitTemplate rabbitTemplate(
            ConnectionFactory connectionFactory){
        RabbitTemplate template = new
                        RabbitTemplate(connectionFactory);
        template.execute(new ChannelCallback<Object>() {

                public Object doInRabbit(Channel channel)
                                    throws Exception {

                    channel.getConnection()
                .addShutdownListener(new ShutdownListener() {

                        public void shutdownCompleted(
                          ShutdownSignalException cause) {
                                        // Process the shutdown
                            }

                });

                return null;
            }
        });
        return template;
}
```

You can have only one RabbitTemplate and add the BlockedListener and ShutdownListener to the same code.

More Features

There are a lot of features exposed by the Spring AMQP module, and it would take a whole book just to explain each one of them. I point out some of them in this section:

- *Transactions*: The Spring AMQP allows you to use the @Transactional annotation in your code, so by adding this annotation, the Spring AMQP module sets the channels in transaction mode. It then can do the commit or rollback, depending on the case. You can also specify the transaction manager you want to use by defining a bean:

```
@Transactional
public void processInvoice() {
    String incoming = rabbitTemplate.receiveAndConvert();
    // Do some more database processing...
    String reply = reviewInvoice(incoming);
    rabbitTemplate.convertAndSend(reply);
}
```

- *Multi-Listeners*: Spring AMQP version 1.5.0 and above adds a new way to have one class that processes multiple listeners depending of the type of message (if needed). Take a look at the MultiListenerService code. You can add the methods the
@Payload, @Header, and @Headers annotations if you need to.

```
@Component
@RabbitListener(id="multi", queues = "${apress.amqp.queue}")
public class MultiListenerService {

    @RabbitHandler
    @SendTo("${apress.amqp.reply-exchange-queue}")
    public Order processInvoice(Invoice invoice) {
        Order order = new Order();

        //Process Invoice here...

        order.setInvoice(invoice);
        return order;
    }

    @RabbitHandler
    public Order processInvoiceWithTax(
                    InvoiceWithTax invoiceWithTax) {
        Order order = new Order();

        //Process Invoice with Tax here...

        return order;
    }
```

```
@RabbitHandler
public String itemProcess(
  @Header("amqp_receivedRoutingKey") String routingKey,
  @Payload Item item) {
      //Some Process here...
      return "{\"message\": \"OK\"}";
}

}
```

- *Retries:* Sometimes you will get an error, either by processing the message or by the broker, and you will need to retry at the consumer level. You need to use this feature for that scenario:

```
// Retry for the consumer,
// normally this needs to be set in the container:
// container.setAdviceChain(new Advice[] { interceptor() });
//
@Bean
public StatefulRetryOperationsInterceptor interceptor() {
        return RetryInterceptorBuilder.stateful()
                .maxAttempts(3)
                .backOffOptions(1000, 2.0, 10000)
                .build();
}
```

- Or this:

```
@Bean
RetryOperationsInterceptor interceptor(
        RabbitTemplate template,
  @Value("${apress.amqp.error-exchange:}")String errorExchange,
  @Value("${apress.amqp.error-routing-key}")String
                                errorExchangeRoutingKey) {
        return RetryInterceptorBuilder.stateless()
                    .maxAttempts(3)
                    .recoverer(
                new RepublishMessageRecoverer(template, errorExchange,
                errorExchangeRoutingKey))
                    .build();
}
```

There are more. Take a look at the Spring AMQP project reference to learn more about these awesome features.

Currency Project

You can continue with the currency project and add the necessary logic to provide a way to consume messages about the different market currency rates. You can review all the code; it's ready to go.

Use the demo to send the rate messages (the demo has all necessary code at `http://projects.spring.io/spring-amqp/`).

Summary

This chapter discussed the AMQP model and explained the difference between exchanges, bindings, and queues. It reviewed some simple examples that illustrated the way to create producers and consumers.

You saw some amazing features of the Spring AMQP module and how Spring Boot helps you with the configuration.

One of the benefits of using Spring messaging is that every Spring technology uses the same concept. The way we send messages (producers); the use of the template pattern (`JmsTemplate`, `RabbitTemplate`, etc.); the way we create the listeners (consumers) using interfaces (by implementing a `MessageListener`) or annotations (like `@JmsListener`, `@RabbitListener`, `@SendTo`, and very soon you will see the `@StreamListener`); the way to access the message structure directly with annotations (like `@Payload`, `@Header`, etc.)—they are all similar in construction.

Remember that this is just a tiny bit of what you can do with Spring AMQP, and I would need to write an entire book on Spring AMQP to show you every single feature. You now have the minimum knowledge needed to create awesome AMQP apps.

The next chapter covers publisher/subscriber messaging, but this time using Redis as the main messaging engine.

## CHAPTER 6

Messaging with Redis

This chapter shows you how to use Redis (REmote DIctionary Server) as a message broker with Spring Boot. Redis is an in-memory data structure store that is used as a database, cache, and message broker. It not only stores key-value pairs, but also can be used to store complex data types such as hashes, lists, sets, sorted sets, bitmaps, hyperlogs, and geospatial indexes.

Spring Boot uses the Spring Data module and in particular the Redis one. In other words, in order to use Redis in your project, you must add the `spring-boot-starter-redis` dependency to your `pom.xml` file or to Gradle. You will then have all the necessary dependencies to connect to a Redis server.

Redis as a Message Broker

Redis not only provides a way to store data structures, but also implements the publish/subscribe messaging paradigm. Previous chapters explained this paradigm with JMS.

The important part here shows you how to interact with Redis and enable the message broker. Redis has the knowledge of a channel, where a message will be sent by the publisher. It will be consumed by subscribers that are interested in one or more of the channels. As you can see, the `channel` keyword is used in Redis. The channels in Redis are the topics in the JMS world.

Redis has several commands that allow you to interact with the publish/subscribe feature:

- SUBSCRIBE: Tells Redis to subscribe to a particular channel or channels. For example:

  ```
  127.0.0.1:6379> SUBSCRIBE spring-boot-chat
  ```

  You can subscribe to multiple channels at once by listing them separated by spaces.

- UNSUBSCRIBE: Unsubscribes from a channel. This command doesn't require a parameter.

- PUBLISH: Publishes a message by specifying the channels (as first parameter) and the actual message. For example:

  ```
  127.0.0.1:6379> PUBLISH spring-boot-chat "Hi there"
  ```

© Felipe Gutierrez 2017

F. Gutierrez, *Spring Boot Messaging*, DOI 10.1007/978-1-4842-1224-0_6

- PSUBSCRIBE: This command is the same as SUBSCRIBE, but accepts a pattern for multiple channels. For example:

  127.0.0.1:6379> PSUBSCRIBE currency.*

  This example will subscribe to any channel that starts with currency, such as currency.us, currency.asia.jp, currency.eu.gb, and so on.

- PUNSUBSCRIBE: Unsubscribes using pattern matching. For example:

  127.0.0.1:6379> PUNSUBSCRIBE currency.asia.*

- PING: Returns a PONG if no argument is provided. Normally you use this to test if the connections are still alive.

Just to give it a try, make sure you have Redis installed and it's up and running. (You can download it from https://redis.io/download.) Open a new terminal window and use the redis-cli command to interact with Redis. See Figure 6-1.

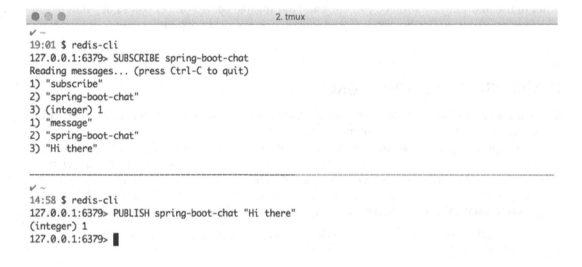

Figure 6-1. *Redis interaction with the publish/subscribe commands*

Figure 6-1 shows you a simple way to interact with Redis and determine how easy it is to subscribe and publish a message.

This chapter does not talk about Redis clustering or about sentinels, sharding, and so forth. It covers messaging. Many customers use Redis extensively as a messaging broker and as a web session management tool for real-time data analysis. The chapter starts by using Spring Boot and Redis for messaging.

Publish/Subscribe Messaging with Redis

As mentioned, Spring Boot will use the power of Spring Data Redis, which is very similar to the Spring JMS, which you are familiar with. Spring Boot will configure the necessary components, such as the connection, the database to use (the 0 index DB by default), cluster nodes if any, the pool, the sentinel, the timeouts, etc. Remember simply adding `spring-boot-starter-redis` enables the Redis auto-configuration.

The Spring Data Redis module has two main areas for messaging—the production or publication and the consumption or subscription of messages. For message publication, it uses the RedisTemplate<K,V> class (it use the template design pattern) and for subscription, it has a dedicated asynchronous message listener container (an MDP—message-driven pojo). For synchronous messages, it uses a RedisConnection interface contract. The following sections cover only the asynchronous subscription.

In this chapter, we are going to work with two projects: `redis-demo` and `rest-api-redis`. The `redis-demo` project has all the necessary code to complete and complement the currency project.

Subscriber

As a Redis subscriber you can subscribe to one or multiple channels (or topics) by using a fixed name or by using pattern matching. The Spring Data Redis module offers a way to do low-level subscriptions via the RedisConnection. This includes the subscribe and pSubscribe methods.

A low-level subscription needs a way to deal with connections and thread management for simple listeners. Now imagine having multiple listeners. You might think it would be a hassle to implement this functionality, but Spring Data Redis includes the RedisMessageListenerContainer class, which does all the heavy lifting and supports the message-driven pojos (MDPs). In other words, you can create your own class and method to receive the message and process it. This means that you need to use the MessageListenerAdapter class in order to use this feature. Don't worry too much, this is what I'm going to show you next.

Open the redis-demo project and review the com.apress.messaging.config.RedisConfig class, shown in Listing 6-1.

Listing 6-1. com.apress.messaging.config.RedisConfig.java

```java
@Configuration
@EnableConfigurationProperties(SimpleRedisProperties.class)
public class RedisConfig {

    @Bean
    public RedisMessageListenerContainer
        container(RedisConnectionFactory connectionFactory,
                    MessageListenerAdapter listenerAdapter,
                @Value("${apress.redis.topic}") String topic) {

        RedisMessageListenerContainer container = new
                            RedisMessageListenerContainer();
            container.setConnectionFactory(connectionFactory);
            container.addMessageListener(listenerAdapter,
                    new PatternTopic(topic));
```

```
        return container;
    }

    @Bean
    MessageListenerAdapter listenerAdapter(
                                Subscriber subscriber) {
        return new MessageListenerAdapter(subscriber);
    }
}
```

Listing 6-1 shows you the configuration that we are going to use in order to subscribe to a channel. Let's see the code in more detail:

- RedisMessageListenerContainer: This is a class that does all the heavy lifting and acts as a message listener container that will receive messages from the Redis channel (topic). You need to set the connection factory and the message listener that will process the message received. Remember that this listener container is responsible for all the threading and message dispatching.

- RedisConnectionFactory: This interface is necessary for the RedisMessageListenerContainer and it holds all the information about the Redis connections. Because it is part of the method, Spring will auto-wire this, so you don't need to create it by hand. Behind the scenes, Spring Boot takes care of this configuration for you.

- MessageListenerAdapter: This class is an adapter that delegates the incoming message to a declared class that is complaint with MessageListener signatures. You can see that this is being set by calling the container.addMessageListener method and passing as parameters the subscriber (listenerAdapter - MessageListenerAdapter) and topic (PatternTopic) where it will subscribe.

- PatternTopic: This is a class and is one of the parameters that the message listener needs. It normally holds the name of the topic or the name pattern that will be used to subscribe to the right channel.

Next, let's look at the Subscriber class. Open the com.apress.messaging.redis.Subscriber class, as shown in Listing 6-2.

Listing 6-2. com.apress.messaging.redis.Subscriber.java

```
@Component
public class Subscriber {

        public void handleMessage(String message){
                // Process message here ...
        }

}
```

Listing 6-2 shows you the Subscriber class with only one required method (handleMessage). The Subscriber class is an adapter for a message delegation. In other words, MessageListenerAdapter is compliant with the following signatures:

```
void handleMessage(String message);
void handleMessage(Map message);
void handleMessage(byte[] message);
void handleMessage(Serializable message);

//You can get the channel or the pattern used
void handleMessage(Serializable message, String channel);
void handleMessage(byte[] bytes, String pattern);

//You can have your own object
void handleMessage(MyOwnDomainObject obj);
```

There may be times when your adapter class will have more methods that do extra processing or are being called from the outside. In these cases, you can let the MessageListenerAdapter class know what method you want to use by adding an extra parameter in its constructor. For example:

```
@Component
public class Subscriber {

        public void shipping(Order order){
                // Process order here ...
        }

        //This method is used as listener for Redis topics
        public void processTicket(String message){
                // Process message here ...
        }

        // ... more methods

}

// RedisConfig.java
@Bean
MessageListenerAdapter listenerAdapter(Subscriber subscriber) {
  return new MessageListenerAdapter(subscriber,"processTicket");
}
```

Add the name of the method that you will use for processing the incoming message from the Redis topic to the constructor; in this example, that's the processTicket method.

As you can see, the benefit of using a MessageListenerAdapter is that you have no dependencies in your POJO class, making your application more extensible.

Publisher

This section covers publishing messages to the channels (topics). To publish a message in Redis, you have two options. You can use the low-level RedisConnection class or the high-level RedisTemplate class (remember, it's very similar to JmsTemplate and RabbitTemplate). Both interfaces provide the publish method connection.publish(msg, channel). You must determine the channel (the topic) as well.

The benefit of using RedisTemplate is that you have a way to define serialization/deserialization strategies. This method hides the complexity of calling raw methods and is thread-safe.

Let's jump into the code. Open the com.apress.messaging.RedisDemoApplication class shown in Listing 6-3.

Listing 6-3. com.apress.messaging.RedisDemoApplication.java

```
@SpringBootApplication
public class RedisDemoApplication {

    public static void main(String[] args) {
        SpringApplication.run(RedisDemoApplication.class, args);
    }

    @Bean
    CommandLineRunner sendMessage(StringRedisTemplate template,
                @Value("${apress.redis.topic}")String topic){
        return args -> {
          template.convertAndSend(topic,
                    "Hello Redis with Spring Boot!");
        };
    }
}
```

Listing 6-3 shows the main application class. As you know, once Spring Boot finalizes the auto-configuration, it will execute the sendMessage method. This method will auto-wire the StringRedisTemplate and the topic with the provided values in the application.properties file with the apress.redis.topic=spring-boot-chat key. Then it will use the template to send a message, by using the template.convertAndSend method that accepts the topic and the message as its parameters.

You normally need to use the RedisTemplate, but in this case, we are using the StringRedisTemplate. We do this because RedisTemplate is defined as RedisTemplate<K,V> where the K is the Redis key type (normally a string) and the V is the Redis value type (it will be the message). Then, StringRedisTemplate is a subclass that uses the string. In other words, it is like creating a RedisTemplate<String,String> object.

What is interesting here is that StringRedisTemplate defines multiple string serializers for different operations that apply to different data structures, such as the Set and Hash key/values.

Now, if you run the project (remember to have the redis-server up and running), you will see the subscriber logs shown in Figures 6-2, 6-3, and 6-4.

```
2017-01-19 11:27:26.545  INFO 22714 --- [    container-2] RedisAudit
=====================================
[BEFORE]
 Class: com.apress.messaging.redis.Subscriber
Method: handleMessage
Params:
> arg0: Hello Redis with Spring Boot!

[AFTER]
Return: void/null
=====================================
```

Figure 6-2. *Project logs*

Figure 6-2 shows you the logs. The RedisAudit class that has an Around AOP advice generates those logs. As you can see, it's using the Subscriber class (listener adapter) and the handleMessage method that received the string message.

Figure 6-3 shows the terminal with the Redis client. The monitor is shown before executing the code, just to determine if Redis accepts the messages. As you can see, Redis is showing the commands executed in the redis-server—in this case, PSUBSCRIBE and PUBLISH and of course a PING command to check out the connections between the client and the server.

```
●●●                              2. tmux
✔ ~
19:02 $ redis-cli
127.0.0.1:6379> monitor
OK
1484850446.521677 [0 127.0.0.1:50476] "PSUBSCRIBE" "spring-boot-chat"
1484850446.532828 [0 127.0.0.1:50477] "PUBLISH" "spring-boot-chat" "Hello Redis with Spring Boot!"
1484850475.951827 [0 127.0.0.1:50477] "PING"
1484850505.953687 [0 127.0.0.1:50477] "PING"
▉
```

```
[base] 0:redis-server  1:monitor* 2:ruby-client  3:tmp-        "pivotal-es.local" 11:28 19-Jan-17
```

Figure 6-3. *The redis-cli monitor command*

Figure 6-4 shows you another terminal window, where we subscribe to the `spring-boot-chat` channel/topic. After running the project, it will print the message. This is another way to make sure your `redis-server` is running and you can have multiple subscribers to a channel/topic.

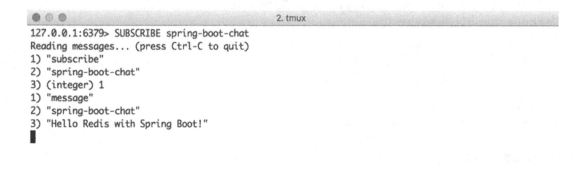

Figure 6-4. *redis-cli subscribe*

JSON Serialization

Now, going back to serialization/deserialization, recall that we are working with the JSON format. What do you need to do to make the publisher/subscribe use JSON and serialize/deserialize it into a custom object back and forth?

If you follow the same idea from the previous modules (JMS and RabbitMQ), answering this question is easier because you can apply the same concepts here.

Let's start by modifying the `RedisConfig` class, as shown in Listing 6-4.

Listing 6-4. com.apress.messaging.config.RedisConfig.java

```
@Configuration
@EnableConfigurationProperties(SimpleRedisProperties.class)
public class RedisConfig {

    @Bean
    public RedisMessageListenerContainer container(
                    RedisConnectionFactory connectionFactory,
                        MessageListenerAdapter rateListenerAdapter,
                @Value("${apress.redis.rate}") String topic) {
```

```
        RedisMessageListenerContainer container =
                    new RedisMessageListenerContainer();
            container.setConnectionFactory(connectionFactory);
container.addMessageListener(rateListenerAdapter,
                                new PatternTopic(topic));
        return container;
    }

    @Bean
    MessageListenerAdapter rateListenerAdapter(
                        RateSubscriber subscriber) {
        MessageListenerAdapter messageListenerAdapter =
                new MessageListenerAdapter(subscriber);
        messageListenerAdapter.setSerializer(
            new Jackson2JsonRedisSerializer<>(Rate.class));
        return messageListenerAdapter;
    }

    @Bean
    RedisTemplate<String, Rate>
     redisTemplate(RedisConnectionFactory connectionFactory){

        RedisTemplate<String,Rate> redisTemplate =
                        new RedisTemplate<String,Rate>();
            redisTemplate.setConnectionFactory(connectionFactory);
        redisTemplate.setDefaultSerializer(
            new Jackson2JsonRedisSerializer<>(Rate.class));
        redisTemplate.afterPropertiesSet();
        return redisTemplate;
    }
}
```

Listing 6-4 shows you the modified RedisConfig class. Comparing it to the previous version, what is the difference? The RedisMessageListenerContainer bean is the same, except that now we are also using the rateListenerAdapter bean. Let's review this listing:

- MessageListenerAdapter: This is the same as before, but here we are setting a new class adapter, in this case the RateSubscriber. It's important to note that we are setting a serializer by calling the setSerializer method and we are instantiating a Jackson2JsonRedisSerializer object using the Rate class as an object mapper.

- RedisTemplate<String,Rate>: As you can see, we are defining this bean to return a RedisTemplate, where the key is a string and the value is the Rate class. Note also that we are setting a serializer by calling the setDefaultSerializer method and we are using the same class as before, Jackson2JsonRedisSerializer.

Look at the RateSubscriber class, shown in Listing 6-5.

Listing 6-5. com.apress.messaging.redis.RateSubscriber.java

```
@Component
public class RateSubscriber {

    public void handleMessage(Rate rate){
        // Process message here ...
    }
}
```

Listing 6-5 shows you the RateSubscriber class. Nothing has changed from the previous example. The handleMessage method will receive a Rate message. Now, let's look at the publisher, shown in Listing 6-6.

Listing 6-6. com.apress.messaging.RedisDemoApplication.java

```
@SpringBootApplication
public class RedisDemoApplication {

    public static void main(String[] args) {
        SpringApplication.run(RedisDemoApplication.class, args);
    }

    @Bean
    CommandLineRunner sendRateMessage(
                RedisTemplate<String, Rate> template,
                @Value("${apress.redis.rate}")String topic){

        return args -> {
                template.convertAndSend(topic,
                        new Rate("MX",21.17F,new Date()));
        };
    }
}
```

Listing 6-6 shows you the main application. Compare this class to the previous version; what changed? We are using the RedisTemplate class and using the Rate as the value. We are also using the Rate class as a message by creating a new rate.

Now you can run your project and see the logs. See Figures 6-5, 6-6, and 6-7.

Figure 6-5 shows you the logs where the RateSubscriber is processing the message. Remember, behind the scenes, a serialization/deserialization is happening in order to get the object.

```
2017-01-18 10:33:14.781  INFO 95657 --- [    container-2] RedisAudit
====================================
[BEFORE]
 Class: com.apress.messaging.redis.RateSubscriber
Method: handleMessage
Params:
> arg0: Rate [code=MX, rate=21.17, date=2017-01-18]

[AFTER]
Return: void/null
====================================
```

Figure 6-5. *RateSubscriber logs*

Figure 6-6 shows you a terminal with a Redis client monitor. The idea is to see that the published method is a string in a JSON format, which means that the Jackson2JsonRedisSerializer performed the serialization of the Rate class.

```
● ● ●                                    2. tmux
11:50 $
✔ ~
11:50 $ redis-cli
127.0.0.1:6379> monitor
OK
1484851872.652987 [0 127.0.0.1:50709] "COMMAND"
1484851901.845622 [0 127.0.0.1:50709] "SUBSCRIBE" "currency-rate"
1484851920.423009 [0 127.0.0.1:50723] "PSUBSCRIBE" "currency-rate"
1484851920.459250 [0 127.0.0.1:50724] "PUBLISH" "currency-rate" "{\"code\":\"MX\",\"rate\":21.17,\"date\":1484851920427}"
1484851949.838610 [0 127.0.0.1:50724] "PING"
▮
```

```
[base] 0:redis-server  1:monitor* 2:ruby-client- 3:tmp                    "pivotal-es.local" 11:52 19-Jan-17
```

Figure 6-6. *redis-cli monitor*

Figure 6-7 shows you a terminal with a subscriber to the currency-rate channel/topic. Note that this subscriber received the Rate message as a JSON string format.

Figure 6-7. *redis-cli subscriber*

If you compare these results with the previous Spring modules (JMS and AMQP), you'll see that we are doing the same thing. Even though this Spring Data Redis module doesn't have annotations to simplify the publish/subscribe pattern, it's easy to get this up and running in no time.

The Currency Project

You now have all the necessary information to complete the currency project. Take a look at the `RateRedisSubscriber`, `RateRedisConfig`, and the `RateRedisProperties` classes to start. You can reuse the demo project to publish messages to the channel/topic.

■ **Note**   Remember that it's important to have the `redis-server` up and running before you run the currency project.

Summary

This chapter talked about the publish/subscribe messaging pattern and showed that Redis provides this functionality out-of-the-box. It's very easy to use. The chapter showed you how Spring Boot helps configure your publisher and subscriber with ease, simply by adding `spring-boot-starter-redis`.

You saw how to publish and listen for incoming messages and you saw that the Spring Data Redis module uses very a similar way as a publisher and subscriber by using the `RedisTemplate` (the same behavior as the Spring JMS and Spring AMQP modules).

Even though this chapter is short, it gives you a starting point for using Redis as an in-memory message broker.

The next chapter covers WebSockets, which is another way to do messaging using Spring Boot.

CHAPTER 7

■ ■ ■

Web Messaging

This chapter covers WebSockets with Spring Boot and describes how this technology can help you implement messaging across apps or even across multiple instances of the same application.

When talking about web applications, we can say that REST is another way to do messaging, and it is. In this chapter, we are going to focus on a stateful way of communicating, which is what WebSockets brings to the table.

WebSockets

WebSockets is a protocol that enables two-way communication, and it's normally used in web browsers. This protocol starts by using a handshake (normally a HTTP request) and then sends a basic message frame (a protocol switch) over TCP. The idea of the WebSockets is to avoid multiple HTTP connections like the AJAX (XMLHttpRequest) or the iframe and the long polling. See Figure 7-1.

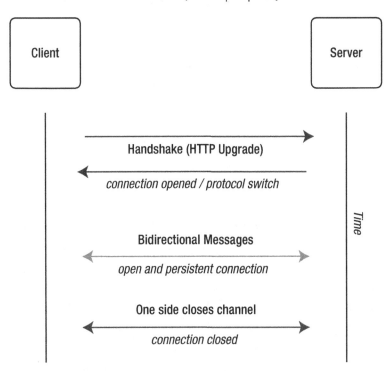

Figure 7-1. *TCP/WebSockets*

© Felipe Gutierrez 2017 93
F. Gutierrez, *Spring Boot Messaging*, DOI 10.1007/978-1-4842-1224-0_7

Using WebSockets with Spring

Before we get into how to use WebSockets with Spring Boot, it's important to know that not all the browsers support this technology. Visit http://caniuse.com/websockets to find out which browsers are WebSockets-ready.

The Spring Framework version 4 includes a new spring-websocket module that supports WebSockets; it's also compatible with the Java specification JSR-356. This module also has fallback options that simulate the WebSockets API when necessary (remember that not all the browsers support WebSockets). It uses the SockJS protocol for this task. You can get more information about it at https://github.com/sockjs/sockjs-protocol.

It's also worth mentioning that after the initial handshake (the HTTP, where we use SockJS), the communications switch to a TCP connection (meaning that you are sending just a stream of bytes—either text or binary). Therefore, you can use any type of messaging architecture, like async or event-driven messaging. At this level, you can use sub-protocols like STOMP (Simple/ Streaming Text Oriented Message Protocol), which allows you to have a better messaging format that the client and server can understand. See Figure 7-2.

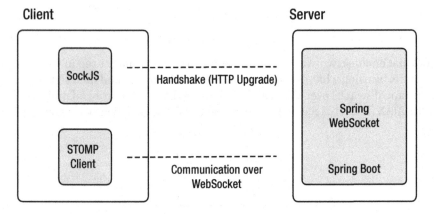

Figure 7-2. *WebSockets with Spring*

Figure 7-2 shows how to implement WebSockets using Spring and the components needed on the client side.

Low-Level WebSockets

Before we jump into the fallback options (SockJS) and sub-protocols (STOMP), let's see how can we use Spring Boot with a low-level WebSockets.

In the book's source code, go to the Chapter 7 and open the two projects (you can import them into your favorite IDE or use any text editor). In the following section, we are going to work with the websocket-demo project.

Let's start by analyzing the configuration. In order to use low-level WebSockets communications, we need to implement the org.springframework.web.socket.config.annotation. WebSocketConfigurer interface. Open the com.apress.messaging.config.LlWebSocketConfig class, as shown in Listing 7-1.

Listing 7-1. com.apress.messaging.config.LlWebSocketConfig.java

```
@Configuration
@EnableWebSocket
public class LlWebSocketConfig implements WebSocketConfigurer{

    LlWebSocketHandler handler;

    public LlWebSocketConfig(LlWebSocketHandler handler){
        this.handler = handler;
    }

    @Override
    public void registerWebSocketHandlers(
                            WebSocketHandlerRegistry registry) {
            registry.addHandler(this.handler, "/llws");
    }

}
```

Listing 7-1 shows you the configuration needed to enable WebSockets in Spring. Remember, the way we are configuring this class is to have a low-level WebSockets communication. Let's review the components that are used:

- @EnableWebSocket: This is necessary to enable and configure WebSockets requests.

- WebSocketConfigurer: This is an interface that defines callback methods to configure the WebSockets request handling. Normally you are required to implement the registerWebSocketHandlers method.

- registerWebSocketHandlers: This method needs to be implemented by adding the handlers that will be used for the WebSockets processing request. In this method, we are registering a handler (LlWebSocketHandler) instance and passing the endpoint used for the handshake and communication.

- WebSocketHandlerRegistry: This an interface used to register a WebSocketHandler implementation. We are going to use a TextWebSocketHandler implementation and look at its code in the next section.

As you can see, it's very simple to configure a low-level WebSockets using Spring. Next, let's open the com.apress.messaging.web.socket.LlWebSocketHandler class. See Listing 7-2.

Listing 7-2. com.apress.messaging.web.socket.LlWebSocketHandler.java

```java
@Component
public class LlWebSocketHandler extends TextWebSocketHandler{

    @Override
    public void afterConnectionEstablished(
                    WebSocketSession session) throws Exception {
        super.afterConnectionEstablished(session);
    }

    @Override
    protected void handleTextMessage(
            WebSocketSession session, TextMessage message)
                                        throws Exception {
            System.out.println(">>>> " + message);
        }
}
```

Listing 7-2 shows you the WebSockets handler we are going to use to receive messages from the client. Let's examine this class:

- TextWebSocketHandler: This is a concrete class that implements the WebSocketHandler interface through the AbstractWebSocketHandler class. This implementation is for processing text messages only. We are going to override two methods: afterConnectionEstablished and handleTextMessage.

- afterConnectionEstablished: This method is called when the client successfully connects using the WebSockets protocol. In this method, you can use the WebSocketSession instance to send or receive messages. For now, we are going to use its default behavior, but we will see more in the logs (through the AOP WebSocketsAudit class).

- handledTextMessage: This method receives a WebSocketSession (that we are going to use later) and a TextMessage instance. The TextMessage instance manages the stream of bytes and converts them into a string.

So far, we have implemented the server side, but what about the client? Normally, you will have a web page to do the client's job.

Open the src/main/resources/static/llws.html file, as shown in Listing 7-3.

Listing 7-3. Snippet of llws.html

```html
<script>

$(function(){

        var connection = new
                WebSocket('ws://localhost:8080/llws');
```

```
    connection.onopen = function () {
        console.log('Connected...');
    };

    connection.onmessage = function(event){
        console.log('>>>>> ' + event.data);
        var json = JSON.parse(event.data);
        $("#output").append("<span><strong>"
            + json.user
            + "</strong>: <em>"
            + json.message
            + "</em></span><br/>");
    };

    connection.onclose = function(event){
        $("#output").append("CONNECTION: CLOSED");
    };

    $("#send").click(function(){
        var message = {}
        message["user"] = $("#user").val();
        message["message"] = $("#message").val();

    connection.send(JSON.stringify(message));
    });

});

</script>
```

Listing 7-3 shows just the JavaScript snippet of the important code, which I explain next:

- WebSocket: This is part of the JavaScript engine and it will connect to the specified URI. Note that the schema is ws and that we are using the /llws endpoint, which we specified in the configuration class (see Listing 7-1).

- onopen: This is a callback function that is executed when the connection is established with the server. Note that we are only logging a string to the console.

- onmessage: This is a callback function that is executed when a message is received from the server. In this case, we are parsing an event.data into a JSON object.

- onclose: This is a callback function that is executed when the connection is closed or is lost with the server.

- $.click/send: This is a callback function that is attached to the Send button, and it's called when the button is clicked. Here we are using the send method, which will send a JSON string of the message object.

Next, let's run the websocket-demo project; after it starts, open a browser and go to http://localhost:8080/llws.html. You should see something similar to Figure 7-3.

Figure 7-3. *http://localhost:8080/llws.html*

After you go to llws.html in your browser, take a look at the application logs. You should see something similar to Figure 7-4.

```
=====================================
2017-02-17 13:05:48.002  INFO 73029 --- [nio-8080-exec-5] c.apress.messaging.aop.WebSocketsAudit   :
=====================================
[BEFORE]
 Class: com.apress.messaging.web.socket.LlWebSocketHandler
Method: afterConnectionEstablished
Params:
> arg0: StandardWebSocketSession[id=1, uri=/llws]

[AFTER]
Return: void/null
=====================================
```

Figure 7-4. *The websocket-demo project logs*

Figure 7-4 shows you the logs, whereby the `afterConnectionEstablished` is being called from the `LlWebSocketHandler` class. This means that the client was successfully connected to the server. You can also take a look at the browser's developer console to see the logs displaying the string `Connected....` See Figure 7-5.

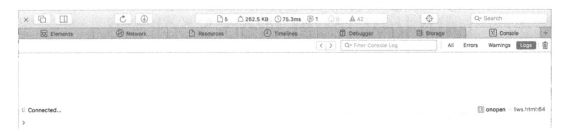

Figure 7-5. *Browser's console*

Next, you can send a message by modifying the user and message inputs from the `llws.html` page and clicking the Send button. After clicking the Send button, you should see something similar to Figure 7-6.

```
>>>> TextMessage payload=[{"user":"s..], byteCount=43, last=true]
```

Figure 7-6. *websocket-demo project logs after clicking Send*

Figure 7-6 shows you the logs after sending the message as well as the print out from the `handleTextMessage` method.

This example shows you how to send a message from the client to the server. Now, let's do a response, an echo, from the server. You need to add something to `handleTextMessage` to handle the reply.

Modify `handleTextMessage` to look like the following:

```
@Override
public void handleTextMessage(
            WebSocketSession session,
            TextMessage message) throws Exception {

    System.out.println(">>>> " + message);

    session.sendMessage(message);
}
```

As you can see, we are using the `session` instance to call `sendMessage`, which means that we are going to reply using the same *session* of the connected client.

Restart the `websocket-demo` project and refresh the `llws.html` page. Then send a message by filling out the user and message inputs. You should see the response in the Echo Messages from the Server panel, as shown in Figure 7-7. Note that if you are using the STS, you only need to wait until the project restarts itself; this is possible thanks to the `spring-boot-devtools`.

Figure 7-7. *Echo server response*

If you stop the application, you will see something like Figure 7-8 in the Echo Messages from the Server panel.

Messages:

CONNECTION: CLOSED

Figure 7-8. *Closed connection*

As you can see, it's very simple to create low-level WebSockets applications. What happens if you need to send a message from a Spring application? In other words, your app needs to be the client. You can add the following code to your application (see Listing 7-4).

Listing 7-4. WebSockets Client—Snippet of the WebSocketDemoApplication Class

```
StandardWebSocketClient client = new StandardWebSocketClient();
ListenableFuture<WebSocketSession> future =
                client.doHandshake(handler,
                        new WebSocketHttpHeaders(),
                        new URI("ws://localhost:8080/ws-server"));
WebSocketSession session = future.get();
WebSocketMessage<String> message =
                new TextMessage("Hello there...");
session.sendMessage(message);
```

Listing 7-4 shows a snippet of what you need to add if you want to create a WebSockets client (instead of HTML web pages). Here we are using StandardWebSocketClient (a low-level WebSockets protocol) and it's manually doing the handshake. It passes the handler some headers and the URI where you will connect. (Note that you can use the previous handler or create your own, and you then can implement the afterConnectionEstablished to check if you were successfully connected.) Then you get a WebSocketSession instance and can send the message.

You can see that using the WebSockets client with Spring classes is a straightforward implementation. Next, let's start using the fallback options with SockJS and the STOMP sub-protocol.

Using SockJS and STOMP

Why do we need to use SockJS and STOMP? Remember that not all the browsers support WebSockets and normally the client and the server must agree on how they will handle messages. Of course, that is not the right way to message, because we want to have a decoupling scenario, where the client is not tied to the server.

SockJS helps emulate WebSockets and performs the initial handshake. Then, by using STOMP, we can reply in an interoperable wire format that allows us to use multiple brokers that support this protocol.

Chat Room Application

We are going to continue using the websocket-demo project, but we are going to work with different files and classes. This example creates a chat room, which is a very common use of the WebSockets technology.

First, let's see how to configure the project will use SockJS and STOMP. Open the com.apress.messaging.config.WebSocketConfig class. See Listing 7-5.

Listing 7-5. com.apress.messaging.config.WebSocketConfig.java

```java
@Configuration
@EnableWebSocketMessageBroker
@EnableConfigurationProperties(SimpleWebSocketsProperties.class)
public class WebSocketsConfig extends
                AbstractWebSocketMessageBrokerConfigurer {

    SimpleWebSocketsProperties props;

    public WebSocketsConfig(SimpleWebSocketsProperties props){
        this.props = props;
    }

    @Override
    public void registerStompEndpoints(
                            StompEndpointRegistry registry) {
            registry.addEndpoint(props.getEndpoint()).withSockJS();
    }

    @Override
    public void configureMessageBroker(
                            MessageBrokerRegistry config) {
        config.enableSimpleBroker(props.getTopic());
        config.setApplicationDestinationPrefixes(
                props.getAppDestinationPrefix());
    }
}
```

Listing 7-5 shows you the configuration needed to use WebSockets with SocksJS and STOMP. Let's review it:

- @EnableWebSocketMessageBroker: This annotation is required to enable broker-backend messaging over WebSockets using a higher-level messaging sub-protocols (SockJS/STOMP).

- AbstractWebSocketMessageBrokerConfigurer: This class implements the WebSocketMessageBrokerConfigurer to configure message handling with simple messaging protocols like STOMP from WebSockets clients.

- registerStompEndpoints: This method is called to register STOMP endpoints, mapping each to a specific URL and configuring the SockJS fallback options.

- StompEndpointRegistry: This is a contract for registering STOMP over WebSockets endpoints. It provides a fluent API to build the registry.

- withSockJS: This method will enable the SockJS fallback options required for the handshake.

- configureMessageBroker: This method is called to configure the message broker options. In this case we are using the MessageBrokerRegistry.

- MessageBrokerRegistry: This instance will help configure all the broker options. We are using enableSimpleBroker, which accepts one or more prefixes to filter destinations targeting the broker. This will be used together with the annotated methods that have the @SendTo annotation. We are also using the setApplicationDestinationPrefixes to configure one or more prefixes to filter destination targeting the application annotated methods. In other words, it will look for methods that are annotated with @MessageMapping.

You can see that we need to add an endpoint, a broker, and prefix paths to configure WebSockets using SockJS and STOMP. Take a look at Figure 7-9.

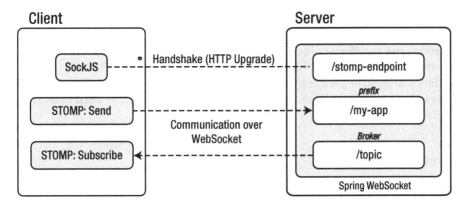

Figure 7-9. *Client/server WebSockets using SockJS and STOMP*

Figure 7-9 shows you a general picture of what the communication will be between the client and the server. Next, open the com.apress.messaging.controller.SimpleController class. See Listing 7-6.

Listing 7-6. com.apress.messaging.controller.SimpleController.java

```
@Controller
public class SimpleController {

    @MessageMapping("${apress.ws.mapping}")
    @SendTo("/topic/chat-room")
    public ChatMessage chatRoom(ChatMessage message) {
        return message;
    }
}
```

Listing 7-6 shows you the receiver and sender by using new annotations. Remember that the project now will run a chat room, so different clients can connect and receive message from other users:

- @MessageMapping: This annotation has to do with the application prefixes, meaning that the client needs to send a message to prefix + mapping. In our case, this is /my-app/chat-room. This annotation is supported by methods of the @Controller classes, and the value can be treated as an ant-style, slash-separated, and path patterns. With this annotation, you have other annotations that can be used as method parameters, including @Payload, @Header, @Headers, @DestinationVariable, and java.security. Principal.

- @SendTo: You already know this annotation; it's the same one we used in the JMS and RabbitMQ chapters. In this case, this annotation is used to send a message to any other destination.

Even though we didn't use the @SubscribeMapping, you can use it in a @Controller annotated class, in a method that you want to use to handle incoming messages. This will normally be useful when you need to get a copy of the response by the @SendTo.

Another utility class that we didn't use is SimpleMessagingTemplate. It can be used to send messages. For example:

```
@Controller
public class AnotherController {

    private SimpMessagingTemplate template;

    @Autowired
    public AnotherController(SimpMessagingTemplate template) {
        this.template = template;
    }

    @RequestMapping(path="/rate/new", method=POST)
    public void newRates(Rate rate) {
        this.template.convertAndSend("/topic/new-rate", rate);
    }

}
```

As you can see, it's very simple to implement the subscriber/publisher model using the WebSockets technology. AnotherController acts as a client as well by sending a message (ChatMessage).

Next, let's see another client. Open the src/main/resources/static/sockjs-stomp.html page. See Listing 7-7.

Listing 7-7. Snippet of sockjs-stomp.html

```
$(function(){
    var socket =
        new SockJS('http://localhost:8080/stomp-endpoint');
    var stompClient = Stomp.over(socket);

    stompClient.connect({}, function (frame) {
        console.log('Connected: ' + frame);

        stompClient.subscribe('/topic/chat-room',
                function (data) {
                    console.log('>>>>> ' + data);
                    var json = JSON.parse(data.body);
                    $("#output")
                        .append("<span><strong>"
                                + json.user
                                + "</strong>: <em>"
                                + json.message
                                + "</em></span><br/>");
                });

    });

    $("#send").click(function(){
        var chatMessage = {}
        chatMessage["user"] = $("#user").val();
        chatMessage["message"] = $("#message").val();

        stompClient.send(
                            "/my-app/chat-room",
                            {},
                            JSON.stringify(chatMessage));
                        });
    });
```

Listing 7-7 shows you the JavaScript client. Let's analyze it:

- SockJS: This is a JavaScript library that emulates the WebSockets protocol. This object is connecting to the /stomp endpoint that was specified on the server side. For more information about this library, visit http://sockjs. org/.

- STOMP: This is a JavaScript library that uses the WebSockets protocol and normally will require the SockJS object. For more information, visit http:// jmesnil.net/stomp-websocket/doc/.

- connect: This is a callback that will be called when the connection is established with the server.

- subscribe: This is a callback that will be called when there is a message at the subscribed destination.

- send: This method will send a message to the destination provided.

This is a very simple way to use SockJS and STOMP in a JavaScript client. Now you are ready to run the websockets-demo project.

■ **Note**   Before you run the websocket-demo project in this section, make sure that the LlWebSocketConfig class is disabled (by commenting it out of the @Configuration and @EnableWebSocket annotations).

Run the project and open a browser. Go to the http://localhost:8080/sockjs-stomp.html web page. You will see something similar to the previous example. If you are curious, you can go to the browser's developer console and see the console logs. See Figure 7-10.

Figure 7-10. *Browser's console log*

Figure 7-10 shows you the connection logs. Now open a second browser window and visit the same URL. The idea is to emulate two clients communicating. Next, send some messages and look at the results. See Figures 7-11 and 7-12.

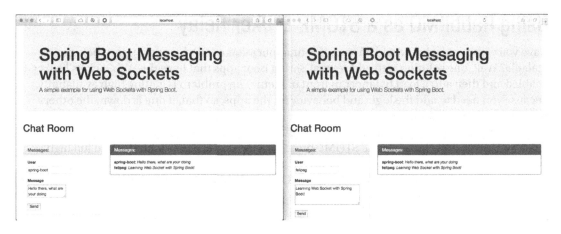

Figure 7-11. *Two browser clients*

```
2017-02-17 16:56:13.765  INFO 80485 --- [boundChannel-22] c.apress.messaging.aop.WebSocketsAudit   :
====================================
[BEFORE]
 Class: com.apress.messaging.controller.SimpleController
Method: chatRoom
Params:
> arg0: ChatMessage [user=spring-boot, message=Hello there, what are your doing, sent=2017-02-17 16:56:13]

[AFTER]
Return: ChatMessage [user=spring-boot, message=Hello there, what are your doing, sent=2017-02-17 16:56:13]
====================================
2017-02-17 16:56:20.820  INFO 80485 --- [boundChannel-25] c.apress.messaging.aop.WebSocketsAudit   :
====================================
[BEFORE]
 Class: com.apress.messaging.controller.SimpleController
Method: chatRoom
Params:
> arg0: ChatMessage [user=felipeg, message=Learning Web Socket with Spring Boot!, sent=2017-02-17 16:56:20]

[AFTER]
Return: ChatMessage [user=felipeg, message=Learning Web Socket with Spring Boot!, sent=2017-02-17 16:56:20]
====================================
```

Figure 7-12. *Application logs*

Figure 7-11 shows two clients sending messages through WebSockets using SockJS and STOMP.

Figure 7-12 shows the SimpleController logs and the ChatMessage is being handled by the chatRoom method (this happened because of the @MessageMapping and @SendTo annotations).

That's how you create a chat room very easily with Spring Boot and the spring-websocket module.

Question: How can you create a SockJS client using Spring? Imagine that you need to send a message to a remote WebSockets connection using STOMP. Look at the code in the WebSocketsDemoApplication class, which is commented out. You will see how to use the SockJSClient and WebSocketsStompClient classes there.

Using RabbitMQ as a STOMP Broker Relay

Have you wondered what would happen if your application needed more support, being more scalable? Well, one solution is to add several Spring Boot apps that have the WebSockets broker enabled and then add a load balancer in front of them. The problem is getting high availability, because you need to add the logic and behavior for the apps, so that, if one is down, the others keep responding to the clients.

The good news is that the spring-websocket module has a way to use an external relay: RabbitMQ. RabbitMQ includes the STOMP protocol as a plugin. It also includes real full high availability and an easy way to set up a cluster.

Follow these steps to add RabbitMQ as a STOMP relay to your application:

1. Make sure to enable the RabbitMQ STOMP plugin:

```
$ rabbitmq-plugins enable rabbitmq_stomp
$ rabbitmq-plugins enable rabbitmq_web_stomp
```

2. Add the following dependencies to your pom.xml file.

```
<dependency>
    <groupId>io.projectreactor</groupId>
    <artifactId>reactor-core</artifactId>
</dependency>
<dependency>
    <groupId>io.projectreactor</groupId>
    <artifactId>reactor-net</artifactId>
</dependency>
<dependency>
    <groupId>io.netty</groupId>
    <artifactId>netty-all</artifactId>
    <version>4.1.8.Final</version>
</dependency>
```

3. Configure the WebSocketsConfig class similar to the following code:

```
@Override
public void configureMessageBroker(
                    MessageBrokerRegistry config) {

        config.setApplicationDestinationPrefixes(
                        props.getAppDestinationPrefix());

        config.enableStompBrokerRelay(
                "/topic", "/queue").setRelayPort(61613);

}
```

What is different from the previous version is that now in the `configureMessageBroker` method you are configuring the `enableStompBrokerRelay` (using /topic and /queue) and adding the STOMP port with the `setRelayPort` method (with the value of 61613, the RabbitMQ's STOMP port).

And that's it. You can now use RabbitMQ as a broker relay. Before you run the project, make sure the RabbitMQ broker is up and running. Then you can run the project and use the same `sockjs-stomp.html` web page. The important part here is to keep an eye on the RabbitMQ console to see connections and queues.

Currency Project

Take a look at the `rest-api-websockets` project. You will find the `RateWebSocketsConfig` class, which is very similar to the other project. The idea is that the currency project has a simple WebSockets broker, which will accept any client connection through the WebSockets protocol.

Every time there is a new rate posted, it will send a message to the client's subscribe to the /rate/new endpoint. Take a look at this:

- `RateWebSocketsConfig`: This class has the configuration needed for WebSockets messaging.

- `CurrencyController`: This class in the `addNewRates` method has the following statement:

  `webSocket.convertAndSend("/rate/new", currencyExchange);`

- `src/main/resources/public/index-ws.html`: This web page has the code that defines the client that connects to the server. Take a look; it's very straightforward.

To test it, you just add a simple post to the command line:

```
$ curl -i -X POST -H "Content-Type: application/json" -H "Accept: application/json"
-d '{"base":"USD","date":"2017-02-15","rates":[{"code":"EUR","rate":0.82857,
"date":"2017-02-15"},{"code":"JPY","rate":105.17,"date":"2017-02-15"},
{"code":"MXN","rate":22.232,"date":"2017-02-15"},
{"code":"GBP","rate":0.75705,"date":"2017-02-16"}]}' localhost:8080/currency/new
```

You can also use any other REST client, such as POSTMAN: https://www.getpostman.com/. After posting the new rate, you will see the Rates in the panel, as shown in Figure 7-13.

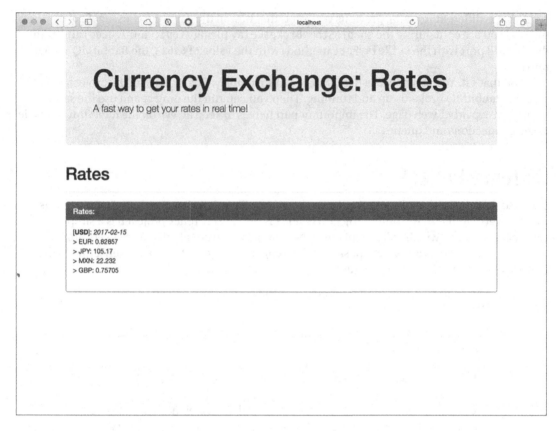

Figure 7-13. *Currency exchange through WebSockets*

Summary

This chapter discussed WebSockets messaging using the `spring-websocket` module and Spring Boot.

You learned how the WebSockets uses an HTTP handshake and then switches to TCP connections. You saw examples of how to create a low-level server/client.

You saw how to use the SockJS and STOMP to facilitate communication for doing async or event-driven messaging. You also learned how to configure RabbitMQ and use it as a STOMP relay. You saw some code in the currency exchange project that sends new rates for any client that connects to this service.

The next chapter shows you how to integrate your code with multiple technologies using the Spring Integration module.

CHAPTER 8

■ ■ ■

Messaging with Spring Integration

This chapter covers one of the best integration frameworks for the Java community, the Spring Integration module. It's of course based on the Spring Framework.

If we look at software development and business needs as a developer or an architect, we are always looking at how to integrate internal and external components and systems into our architecture. We need components that are fully functional, highly available, and easy to maintain and enhance.

The main uses cases that developers and architects face include:

- Creating a system that reliably transfers and analyzes files. Most applications need to read information from a file and process it. Developers need to create robust file systems that save and read data but can also share it and deal with large file sizes.

- Using data in a shared environment. Multiple clients (systems or users) need to have access to the same database or the same table and perform operations on them and deal with inconsistency, duplication, and more.

- Having remote access to different systems is always challenging, from executing remote procedures to sending information. We always want to have this access in real time and in a synchronous way. We must get a response as fast as possible without forgetting that the remote system always needs to be reachable. In other words, the system must be fault tolerant and have high availability.

- Messaging is an important use case that we always want for any system, from a basic internal call to a billions of messages per second sent to remote brokers. We typically handle messaging in a asynchronous way, so we need to deal with concurrency, multi-threading, speed (network latency), high availability, fault tolerance, and more.

How can developers implement all of these use cases? About 14 years ago, two software engineers named Gregor Hohpe and Bobby Woolf wrote the seminal book *Enterprise Integration Patterns: Designing, Building and Deploying Messaging Solutions*, published by Addison-Wesley. This book exposes all the messaging patterns needed to solve these use cases. The book also provides a better understanding of how systems interconnect and work, and how—with application architecture, object-oriented design, and message-oriented design—you can create a robust integration system. I highly recommend you read it.

© Felipe Gutierrez 2017
F. Gutierrez, *Spring Boot Messaging*, DOI 10.1007/978-1-4842-1224-0_8

The following sections show you some of these patterns using the Spring Integration module from the Spring Framework.

Spring Integration Primer

Spring Integration is a simple model for implementing enterprise integration solutions, because it facilitates asynchronous and message-driven design within a Spring Boot application. It implements the Enterprise Integration patterns for creating enterprise, robust, and portable integration solutions.

You can use the Spring Integration module to create components that are loosely coupled for modularity and testability. It helps enforce the separation of concerns between your business and integration logic.

Spring Integration exposes these main components:

- Message: This is a generic wrapper for any Java object. It consists of headers and a payload. The headers normally have important information like IDs, timestamps, correlation IDs, and return addresses. You can add your own information to be used with your business logic. The payload can be any type of data, from an array of bytes, strings, and custom objects—anything. You can find its definition in the `spring-messaging` module, which is in the `org.springframework.messaging` package.

  ```
  public interface Message<T> {
          T getPayload();
          MessageHeaders getHeaders();
  }
  ```

  As you can see, there is nothing to fancy in the `Message` definition.

- Message Channel: You can see a message channel as a pipes and filters architecture, very similar to the command you use in a UNIX system. To use the message channel, you need to have producers and consumers. The producer sends the message to the message channel, where a consumer receives it. See Figure 8-1.

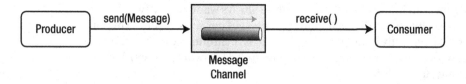

Figure 8-1. *Message channel*

This message channel can follow the messaging patterns discussed in previous chapters—the *point-to-point* and *publish/subscribe* models. Spring Integration offers several message channels, including pollable channels (allow you to have buffered messages within a queue) or subscribable channels for the consumers.

- *Message Endpoint*: A message endpoint is like a filter that will connect the application code to the messaging framework. Most of these endpoints are part of the Enterprise Integration patterns' implementations:

  - *Filter*: A message filter determines when a message should be passed to the output channel.

  - *Transformer*: A message transformer modifies the content or structure of a message and passes it to the output channel.

  - *Router*: A message router decides what to do and where to send the message based on rules. These rules can be in the headers or even in the same payload. This message router has many patterns that can be applied, and I'll show you at least one of them.

  - *Splitter*: A message splitter will accept a message (input channel) and split and return new multiple messages (output channel).

  - *Service Activator*: This is an endpoint that acts as a service by receiving a message (input channel) and processing it. It can end the flow of the integration, return the same message, or send a new one (output channel).

  - *Aggregator*: This message endpoint will receive multiple messages (input channel). It will combine the messages into a new single message (based on a release strategy) and it will send the new message out (output channel).

  - *Channel Adapters*: This is a particular endpoint that connects a message channel to other systems or transports. Spring Integration offers you inbound and outbound adapters. When you need a response, it offers a gateway adapter. You will see that these are the most commonly used. If your solution is looking to connect to RabbitMQ, JMS, FTP, a file system, HTTP, or any other technology, Spring Integration already has the adapter to connect to it without you having to code a client.

It would take a whole new book to describe everything about Spring Integration and each message (message patterns), messaging channels, adapters, and more. If you are interested in this technology, I recommend my *Pro Spring Integration* book from Apress http://www.apress.com/us/book/9781430233459.

The next section describes some of these components and patterns, which should be enough to get you started.

Programming Spring Integration

With Spring Integration, you have several ways configure all the components (Message, Message Channel, and Message Endpoints). You can do it using XML, Java Config classes, annotations, and the new Integration DSL. So far, there is no book that covers DSL (Domain Specific Language), which is that's why I focus a little more on it.

We start with a simple example, just to show what you need to have and do to start with Spring Integration. In the book's source code, open the si-demo project from the Chapter 8 folder. This project includes all the examples found in this chapter.

A Simple Spring Integration Example

Using DSL

We are going to start with the configuration class. Open the com.apress.messsaging.config. SpiSimpleConfiguration class. See Listing 8-1.

Listing 8-1. com.apress.messsaging.config.SpiSimpleConfiguration.java

```
@Configuration
public class SpiSimpleConfiguration {

    @Bean
    public IntegrationFlow simpleFlow(){
        return IntegrationFlows
                        .from(MessageChannels.direct("input"))
                        .filter("World"::equals)
                        .transform("Hello "::concat)
                        .handle(System.out::println)
                        .get();
    }
}
```

Listing 8-1 shows a basic example. This example receives a message from the input channel, filters this message only if it equals the string "World", and then transforms the message by concatenating the string "Hello" and the message "World". It then prints it to the console. All of this is called *integration flow*. Let's take a deeper look inside:

- IntegrationFlow: This is the way we expose the DSL as a bean (this must have a
  @Bean annotation). This class is a factory for the IntegrationFlowBuilder and defines the flow of the integration. It registers all the components like Message Channels, endpoints, etc.

- IntegrationFlows: This class exposes a fluent API that helps build the integration flow. It's easy to incorporate any endpoints like transform, filter, handle, split, aggregate, route, and bridge. With these endpoints, you can use any Java 8 (and above) Lambda expressions as arguments.

- from: This is an overloaded method where you normally pass the MessageSource. In this case, we are passing a direct channel named input.

- filter: This is an overloaded method that will populate a MessageFilter. The MessageFilter delegates to a MessageSelector that will send the message to the filter's output channel only if the selector accepts the Message.

- transform: This method can receive a Lambda expression, but actually receives a GenericTransformer<S,T>, where S is the source and T is the type that it will be converted to. Here, we can use out-of-the-box transformers, including ObjectToJsonTransformer, FileToStringTransformer, etc. In this example, we are just using the contact method from the String class.

- handle: This is an overloaded method that populates a ServiceActivatingHandler. Normally we can use a POJO (Plain Old Java Object), which allows us to receive the message and return a new message or trigger another call. This is a useful endpoint that we are going to see in this chapter and in the next one as a service activator endpoint.

Don't worry too much if this looks different from what you have done in the past for integration solutions; you will get more comfortable as you see more examples and it will get easier.

Next, let's look at the main application, so we can run this example. Open the com.apress. messaging.SpiDemoApplication class. See Listing 8-2.

Listing 8-2. com.apress.messaging.SpiDemoApplication.java

```java
@EnableIntegration
@SpringBootApplication
public class SpiDemoApplication {

    public static void main(String[] args) {
        new SpringApplicationBuilder(SpiDemoApplication.class)
                .web(false)
                .run(args);
    }

    @Bean
    CommandLineRunner process(MessageChannel input){
      return args -> {
          input.send(MessageBuilder.withPayload("World").build());
      };
    }
}
```

Listing 8-2 shows you the main application. Here we are using a new annotation, @ EnableIntegration, which will set up all the Spring Integration beans that we need for our flow. This annotation registers different beans like errorChannel, LoggingHandler, taskScheduler, and more. These beans complement our flow in an integration solution. This annotation is necessary when using a Java configuration, annotations, and DSL in a Spring Boot application.

Note that I added a different way to run a Spring Boot application by using the SpringApplicationBuilder class. If you look at the pom.xml file, you will find that the spring-boot-starter-web dependency is there, meaning that this is a web application. With this example, we don't need the whole embedded server, which is why it's a .web(false) statement.

In the process method, we are requesting a MessageChannel to be injected. Then we use MessageBuilder (a fluent API class), which helps create a message with a payload World.

Remember that in Listing 8-1 we used the `.from(MessageChannels.direct("input"))` statement? This statement will create the message channel "input". This is the channel we are using to send the message to. If you run the application, you should have something similar to Figure 8-2.

```
2017-02-25 08:28:41.174  INFO 12671 --- [ restartedMain] o.s.i.integration.channel.DirectChannel      : Channel application.simple
2017-02-25 08:28:41.174  INFO 12671 --- [ restartedMain] o.s.i.endpoint.EventDrivenConsumer           : started org.springframewor
2017-02-25 08:28:41.174  INFO 12671 --- [ restartedMain] o.s.c.support.DefaultLifecycleProcessor      : Starting beans in phase 21·
GenericMessage [payload=Hello World, headers={id=ede1bd33-7026-6236-4511-76187e8c971d, timestamp=1488036521189}]
2017-02-25 08:28:41.191  INFO 12671 --- [ restartedMain] com.apress.messaging.SpiDemoApplication      : Started SpiDemoApplication
```

Figure 8-2. *SpiDemoApplication logs*

Figure 8-2 shows the logs. You should have a print out. Remember that a message is just about headers and payload, which is why we get a `GenericMessage` class. The final message is `"Hello World"` and there are some headers that include the ID and the timestamp.

Using XML

Next, let's try the same example using XML and learn how to configure the integration flow. Open the `src/main/resources/META-INF/spring/integration/spi-context.xml` file. See Listing 8-3.

Listing 8-3. src/main/resources/META-INF/spring/integration/spi-context.xml

```xml
<int:channel id="input" />

<int:filter   input-channel="input"
              expression="payload.equals('World')"
              output-channel="filter" />
<int:channel id="filter" />

<int:transformer input-channel="filter"
              expression="'Hello '.concat(payload)"
              output-channel="log" />

<int:channel id="log" />

<int:logging-channel-adapter channel="log" />
```

Listing 8-3 shows how to configure the integration flow for XML. I think it's very straightforward. If you are using a STS (Spring Tool Suite) IDE, you can use one of its features, such as the drag-and-drop panel for Spring Integration flows (Integration-Graph). See Figure 8-3.

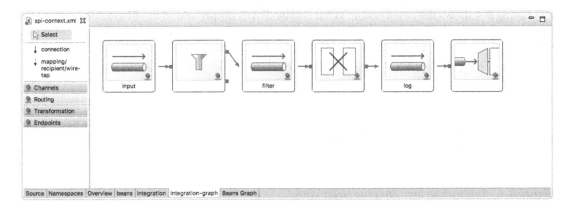

Figure 8-3. *Spring Integration-Graph panel*

Figure 8-3 shows the Integration-Graph panel, where you can create your flows graphically, by dragging and dropping components from the left section. As you can see, there are Channels, Routing, Transformation, Endpoints, and more. Figure 8-3 is actually a translation of the XML. In other words, you can start doing the XML and if you switch to the Integration-Graph, it will show you what you have so far. You can also use this feature to switch to the source, and you will have the XML. A very cool way to create flows, don't you think?

To run this example, you have to comment out the @Configuration annotation from Listing 8-1 (or any other @Component annotation files). Then, the main app (SpiDemoApplication.java) must look like Listing 8-4.

Listing 8-4. com.apress.messaging.SpiDemoApplication.java

```
@ImportResource({"META-INF/spring/integration/spi-context.xml"})
@EnableIntegration
@SpringBootApplication
public class SpiDemoApplication {

    public static void main(String[] args) {
        new SpringApplicationBuilder(SpiDemoApplication.class)
                .web(false)
                .run(args);
    }

    @Bean
    CommandLineRunner process(MessageChannel input){
        return args -> {
        input.send(MessageBuilder.withPayload("World").build());
        };
    }
}
```

Listing 8-4 shows the new version. What changed? We simply added the @ImportResource annotation. This will tell Spring Boot that there is a configuration file that needs to be processed. If you run it (remember to comment out @Configuration from the SpiSimpleConfiguration class), it will print "Hello World" in the logs (by the LoggingHandler class). See Figure 8-4.

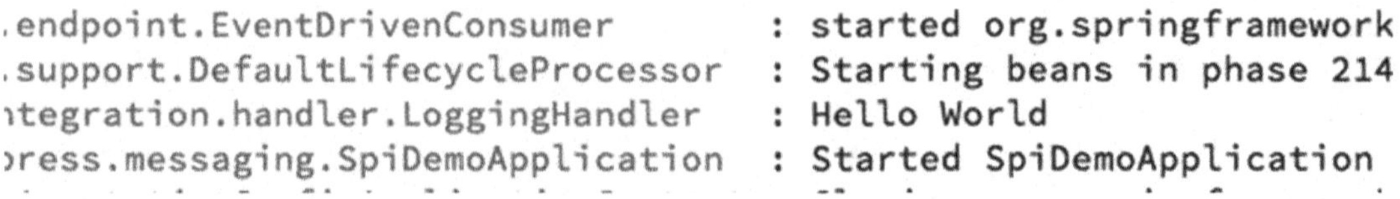

```
.endpoint.EventDrivenConsumer        : started org.springframework
.support.DefaultLifecycleProcessor   : Starting beans in phase 214
itegration.handler.LoggingHandler    : Hello World
ress.messaging.SpiDemoApplication    : Started SpiDemoApplication
```

Figure 8-4. *Application logs showing Hello World*

Using Annotations

Spring Integration includes integration annotations that help you use POJO classes, so that you can add more business logic to your flow and have a little more control.

Open the com.apress.messaging.config.SimpleAnnotationConfiguration class. See Listing 8-5.

Listing 8-5. com.apress.messaging.config.SimpleAnnotationConfiguration.java

```java
@Configuration
public class SimpleAnnotationConfiguration {

    @Bean
    public MessageChannel input(){
        return new DirectChannel();
    }

    @Bean
    public MessageChannel toTransform(){
        return new DirectChannel();
    }

    @Bean
    public MessageChannel toLog(){
        return new DirectChannel();
    }
}

@MessageEndpoint
class SimpleFilter {
    @Filter(inputChannel="input",outputChannel="toTransform")
    public boolean process(String message){
        return "World".equals(message);
    }
}
```

```
@MessageEndpoint
class SimpleTransformer{
    @Transformer(inputChannel="toTransform",outputChannel="toLog")
    public String process(String message){
        return "Hello ".concat(message);
    }
}

@MessageEndpoint
class SimpleServiceActivator{
    @ServiceActivator(inputChannel="toLog")
    public void process(String message){

    }
}
```

Listing 8-5 shows you the same flow, now using the integration annotations. Let's look at it in detail:

- MessageChannel: This is an interface that defines methods for sending messages.

- DirectChannel: This is a message channel that invokes a single subscriber for each message sent. This is normally used when you don't require a message queue.

- @MessageEndpoint: This is a useful annotation that marks a class as an endpoint.

- @Filter: This annotation marks a method to perform the functionality of a message filter. Normally you need to return a Boolean value.

- @Transformer: This annotation marks a method to perform the functionality of transforming a message, its header, or the payload.

- @ServiceActivator: This annotation marks a method as being capable of handling a message. In this example, we just ended the flow. You will see some output from this method thanks to the AOP logs included in this example.

To run this example, just comment out the @ImportResource annotation from the main class and that's it. You should have logs similar to what's shown in Figure 8-5.

```
2017-02-25 14:48:46.608  INFO 23322 --- [  restartedMain]
===================================
[BEFORE]
 Class: com.apress.messaging.config.SimpleFilter
Method: process
Params:
> arg0: World

[AFTER]
Return: true
===================================
2017-02-25 14:48:46.613  INFO 23322 --- [  restartedMain]
===================================
[BEFORE]
 Class: com.apress.messaging.config.SimpleTransformer
Method: process
Params:
> arg0: World

[AFTER]
Return: Hello World
===================================
2017-02-25 14:48:46.620  INFO 23322 --- [  restartedMain]
===================================
[BEFORE]
 Class: com.apress.messaging.config.SimpleServiceActivator
Method: process
Params:
> arg0: Hello World

[AFTER]
Return: void/null
===================================
```

Figure 8-5. *Application logs for this example*

Figure 8-5 shows you the logs for each step where the configuration exposes the filter, the transformer, and the service activator endpoints. I used separate classes here, but of course you can use only one and expose all your methods with their own annotations.

Using Java Config

Using Java Config is very similar to what you just did, so you can simply change the last part of the flow. Comment out the SimpleServiceActivator message endpoint and add the following code to the end of the SimpleAnnotationConfiguration class:

```
@Bean
@ServiceActivator(inputChannel = "toLog")
public LoggingHandler logging() {
    LoggingHandler adapter = new
                    LoggingHandler(LoggingHandler.Level.INFO);
    adapter.setLoggerName("SIMPLE_LOGGER");
    adapter.setLogExpressionString
                    ("headers.id + ': ' + payload");
    return adapter;
}
```

This code will create a LoggingHandler (this is the same object that the XML will generate from the logging-channel-adapter tag). It will log the SIMPLE_LOGGER message with the header's ID and the payload, in this case the "Hello World" message. Now try to send different words and see if the filter works, or try to change the transformer.

I know that this is a trivial example, but it should give you an idea of how Spring Integration works and how it can be configured. Clients often ask whether they can mix configurations. Absolutely! You are going to see examples of that very soon.

File Integration Example

Next, let's see how can you can integrate file reading, which is a very common task of integration systems. Remember that this is one of the most common use cases. Start by opening the com.apress.messaging.config.SpiFileConfiguration class. It should look like Listing 8-6.

Listing 8-6. com.apress.messaging.config.SpiFileConfiguration.java

```
@Configuration
@EnableConfigurationProperties(SpiProperties.class)
public class SpiFileConfigutation {

    private SpiProperties props;
    private PersonConverter personConverter;

    public SpiFileConfigutation(SpiProperties props,
                    PersonConverter personConverter){
        this.props = props;
        this.personConverter = personConverter;
    }
```

```
@Bean
public IntegrationFlow fileFlow(){
    return IntegrationFlows
    .from(Files.inboundAdapter(new File
                                    (this.props.getDirectory())
                .preventDuplicates(true)
                .patternFilter(
                        this.props.getFilePattern()),
                e -> e.poller(Pollers.fixedDelay(5000L)))
    .split(Files.splitter().markers())
    .filter(p -> !(p instanceof FileSplitter.FileMarker))
    .transform(Transformers.converter(personConverter))
    .handle("simpleMessageHandler","process")
    .get();
    }
}
```

Listing 8-6 shows you the integration flow we are going to use in this example. This flow reads a file's contents (from the file system), converts the content into an object (in this case into a Person object), and handles the message for any extra logic. Let's analyze this process in detail:

- from: This is an overloaded method where you normally pass the MessageSource. In this case, we are passing two values— the Files.inboundAdapter and a Consumer that receives a SourcePollingChannelAdapterSpec. In this case, we are using a Lambda expression to poll the file system for new files every five seconds, by using the Pollers class.

- Files: This is a protocol adapter that works out of the box. You just need to configure it. This adapter is used to pick up files from the file system. The Files class belongs to the Spring Integration Java DSL and provides several useful methods:

  - inboundAdapter: This adapter includes a fluent API that returns a FileInboundChannelAdapterSpec that has methods like the following:

    - preventDuplicates: You can avoid reading the same file more than once by setting this to true.

    - patternFilter: This will help look for files have a certain name pattern.

  In this example, we just read from the directory (from the apress.spi.directory property value) and the name based on the pattern (from the apress.spi.file-pattern property value), both from the SpiProperties class.

- split: This method call indicates that the parameter (it could be a bean, service, handler, etc.) can split into a single message or message payload and produce multiple messages or payloads. In this case, we are using a FileMarker that delimits the file data when there is a sequential file process.

- filter: Because we are using markers to see each message start and end, we will receive the content of the file as a `FileMarker` start, then the actual content, and finally the `FileMarker` end. That's why we are saying, just pass me the payload or content, not the marker.

- transform: Here we are using a `Transformers` class that transforms a message. Here we are using a custom converter, which you can look at the code in the `com.apress.messaging.integration.PersonConverter.java` class.

- handle: Here we are using a class that will handle the message by passing as the first parameter the name of the bean (`simpleMessageHandler`) and the method that will take care of the process (`process`; you can look at the code in the `com.apress.messaging.integration.SimpleMessageHandler.java` class). The `SimpleMessageHandler` class is just a POJO marked with the `@Component` annotation.

■ **Note**   The Spring Integration Java DSL currently supports the following protocol adapter classes: `Amqp`, `Jms`, `Files`, `Sftp`, `Ftp`, `Http`, `Kafka`, `Mail`, `Scripts`, and `Feed`. These classes are in the `org.springframework.integration.dsl.*` package.

To run the code, just add the following code to your main class. We are going to comment out some of the past statements. It should look like this code:

```
@EnableIntegration
@SpringBootApplication
public class SpiDemoApplication {

    public static void main(String[] args) {
        new SpringApplicationBuilder(SpiDemoApplication.class)
                .web(false)
                .run(args);
    }
}
```

Before you run this example, make sure you have the `contacts.txt` file, which contains the name, date of birth, phone, e-mail, and friends (a Boolean type to identify if this person is a friend) data. Once you run it, you should have something similar to the output shown in Figure 8-6.

```
========================================
2017-02-26 12:06:52.953  INFO 59460 --- [ask-scheduler-1] com.apress.messaging.aop.SpiAudit        :
========================================
[BEFORE]
 Class: com.apress.messaging.integration.PersonConverter
Method: convert
Params:
> arg0: Jim, Wolf, 1999-08-22, +1 285-374-2357, jim.wolf@company.com, true

[AFTER]
Return: Person [first=Jim, last=Wolf, dob=Fri Jan 22 00:08:00 MST 1999, phone=1999-08-22, email=jim.wo
========================================
2017-02-26 12:06:52.954  INFO 59460 --- [ask-scheduler-1] com.apress.messaging.aop.SpiAudit        :
========================================
[BEFORE]
 Class: com.apress.messaging.integration.SimpleMessageHandler
Method: process
Params:
> arg0: GenericMessage [payload=Person [first=Jim, last=Wolf, dob=Fri Jan 22 00:08:00 MST 1999, phone=

[AFTER]
Return: void/null
========================================
```

Figure 8-6. *Application logs*

As you can see, this is a very simple way to use integration with files, by reading its content and doing business logic with the data.

Remember that previously I told you that you can mix some of the ways you configure Spring Integration? What do you need to do if you want to use an annotation to handle the message? You can use the @ServiceActivator annotation as part of the configuration (in the SpiFileConfiguration class):

```
@ServiceActivator(inputChannel="input")
public void process(Person message){

}
```

To use this service activator method, you need to change the flow. Just replace this line:

```
handle("simpleMessageHandler","process")
```

With this one:

```
.channel("input")
```

If you rerun the example, you will get the same results. Note that there is no input channel defined. The best part is that Spring Integration figures out that you need this channel and creates one behind the scenes for you.

File and JDBC Integration Example

Following the previous example, this example shows how to save the content directly into a database, which is also a common integration use case. Open the com.apress.messaging. config.SpiFileToJdbcConfiguration class shown in Listing 8-7.

Listing 8-7. com.apress.messaging.config.SpiFileToJdbcConfiguration.java

```java
@Configuration
@EnableConfigurationProperties(SpiProperties.class)
public class SpiFileToJdbcConfiguration {

    private SpiProperties props;
    private PersonConverter personConverter;

    public SpiFileToJdbcConfigutation(
                        SpiProperties props,
                        PersonConverter personConverter){
        this.props = props;
        this.personConverter = personConverter;
    }

    @Bean
    public IntegrationFlow fileToJdbcFlow(){
        return IntegrationFlows
          .from(Files.inboundAdapter(
                        new File(this.props.getDirectory()))
                        .preventDuplicates(true)
                        .patternFilter(
                                this.props.getFilePattern()),
                        e -> e.poller(Pollers.fixedDelay(5000L)))

            .split(Files.splitter().markers())
            .filter(p -> !(p instanceof FileSplitter.FileMarker))
            .transform(Transformers.converter(personConverter))
            .filter("payload.isFriend()")
            .channel("input")
            .get();
    }
}
```

Listing 8-7 shows you the new integration flow that will read the same contacts.txt file. After it is transformed into a Person object, we add an extra filter, where only the Person that is a friend will persist into the database. If you take a look after the filter is applied, we are sending it to another channel, called input.

Remember that you can mix ways of programming your integration flows. While writing this book, we had version v1.2.1.RELEASE of the Spring Integration Java DSL and, so far, the Spring Integration team hasn't implemented the JDBC protocol adapter. But don't worry, we are going to use XML to save this information to the database. Open the src/main/resources/META-INF/spring/integration/spi-file-to-jdbc.xml file. See Listing 8-8.

Listing 8-8. The spi-file-to-jdbc.xml File

```xml
<int-jdbc:outbound-channel-adapter
                data-source="dataSource"
                channel="input"
                query="insert into person (first,last,dob,phone,email,friend)
                values (:payload.first, :payload.last, :payload.dob, :payload.
                phone, :payload.email, :payload.friend)"
    />
```

Listing 8-8 shows the XML configuration. Let's analyze it:

- `<int-jdbc:outbound-channel-adapter/>`: This is a JDBC protocol adapter, and this tag is used for all the outgoing JDBC operations. It has different attributes:

  - `data-source`: This attribute references a `DataSource`. The `DataSource` includes all the necessary information about the database you want to connect to, including the URL, username, password, and driver. In this case, we are referencing a bean named `dataSource`, but where is this bean defined? That's the beauty of Spring Boot, you don't need to declare it. If you look at the `pom.xml` file, you will find that one of these dependencies is the H2 database engine. This means that Spring Boot (because it's an opinionated runtime) will configure the H2 (in-memory database) as the default database.

  - `channel`: This attribute is the input channel where the message is coming from. In this case, it's a `Person` object.

  - `query`: This attribute is SQL statement that will be executed when the `Person` object arrives, and if you take a closer look, we are referencing the `Person` object as the payload.

Next, let's see how we are going to add this configuration to the integration flow. You already know how. Open the `com.apress.messaging.SpiDemoApplication` class. See Listing 8-9.

Listing 8-9. com.apress.messaging.SpiDemoApplication.java

```java
@ImportResource("META-INF/spring/integration/spi-file-to-jdbc.xml")
@EnableIntegration
@SpringBootApplication
public class SpiDemoApplication {

    public static void main(String[] args) {
        new SpringApplicationBuilder(SpiDemoApplication.class)
                .web(true)
                .run(args);
    }
}
```

Listing 8-9 shows you version of the main application, and as you knew already, we need to use the @ImportResource annotation to include the XML configuration. This time we are going to enable the web, because the H2 engine provides the /h2-console mapping so that we can take a peek at the database and tables.

If you run the application, you will see the usual logs. Take a look at the http://localhost:8080/h2-console in your browser. See Figures 8-7 and 8-8.

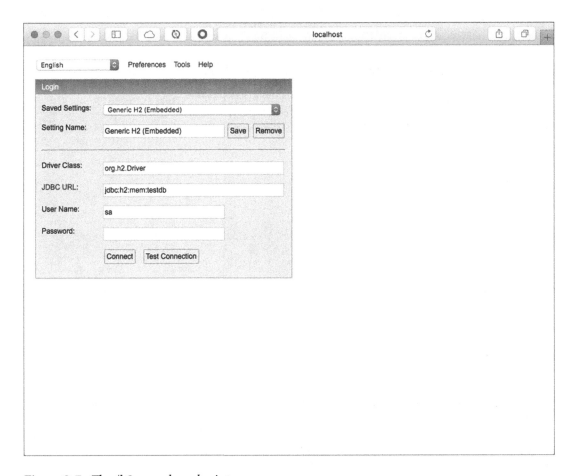

Figure 8-7. *The /h2-console endpoint*

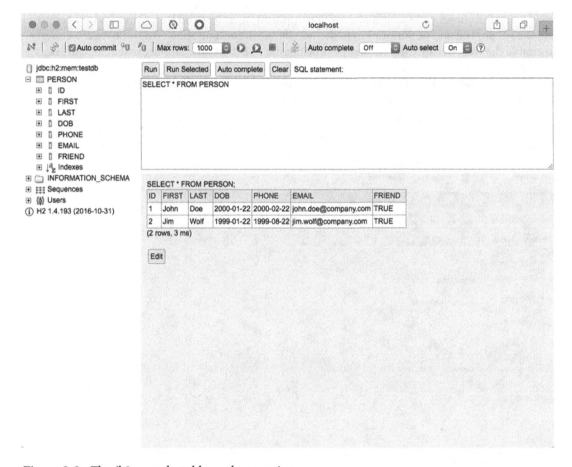

Figure 8-8. *The /h2-console, table, and query view*

Figure 8-7 shows the **/h2-console** endpoint. Spring Boot creates testdb by default and in memory, which is why you have the URL as *jdbc:h2:mem:testdb*.

Figure 8-8 shows the Person table. If you run the SELECT * FROM PERSON SQL statement, you will get that result. You now have only the people from the contacts.txt that are friends (just remember the extra filter we added to the flow).

One question remains: How did Spring Boot tell the H2 engine to create the table called Person? Well, at some point we need to give Spring Boot a little help. If Spring Boot finds in the classpath a file with the name data.sql or schema.sql, it will try to process these files. In the project, you will find the schema.sql file, which defines the table.

AMQP Integration Example

Remember in a previous chapter, we created a producer and consumer using RabbitMQ. In this section, I show you how to use the AMQP protocol adapters from Spring Integration. These adapters are already acting as a producer and consumer. If you need to create a messaging system that involves AMQP, you can use these adapters and they will give you all the flexibility to build a production-ready integration solution. The next example uses the Rate domain object to send rates to the queue.

Open the com.apress.messaging.config.RateConfig class. See Listing 8-10.

Listing 8-10. com.apress.messaging.config.RateConfig.java

```java
@Configuration
@EnableConfigurationProperties(SpiProperties.class)
public class RateConfig {

    @Bean
    public RabbitTemplate rabbitTemplate(
                        ConnectionFactory connectionFactory){
        RabbitTemplate template = new
                                RabbitTemplate(connectionFactory);
         template.setMessageConverter(
                                new Jackson2JsonMessageConverter());
         return template;
    }

    @Bean
    public Queue rateQueue(@Value("${apress.spi.queue}")
                                                        String queue){
        return new Queue(queue,true);
    }

    @Bean
    public MessageChannel amqpChannel() {
        return MessageChannels.direct().get();
    }

    @Bean
    public IntegrationFlow rateFlow(
        RabbitTemplate rabbitTemplate, @Value("${apress.spi.exchange:}") String
exchange,
        @Value("${apress.spi.queue}") String queue){

        return IntegrationFlows
                .from("amqpChannel")
                .handle(Amqp
                        .outboundAdapter(rabbitTemplate)
                        .exchangeName(exchange)
                        .routingKey(queue))
                .get();
    }
}
```

Listing 8-10 shows you the RateConfig class, where we define the integration flow. First, note the familiar objects (Java Config for RabbitMQ), like the RabbitTemplate that sets the Jackson2JsonMessageConverter and the queue creation.

The way the amqpChannel bean is created is new. I'm using the MessageChannels (note the s at the end of the class), which provides a fluent API for channel creation. In this case, it's creating a direct channel.

In the integration flow, I'm using the Amqp (class) protocol adapter. In this case, because we are going to send messages, the outboundAdapter is being used. This adapter will receive the rabbitTemplate, the exchange name, and the routing key. The producer is the Amqp.outboundAdapter protocol adapter.

AMQP Producer

Before you run this example, remember that RabbitMQ needs to be up and running. In your main application, add the following code:

```
@Bean
CommandLineRunner processRate(MessageChannel amqpChannel){
    return args -> {
        amqpChannel.send(
                MessageBuilder.withPayload(new Rate("EUR",0.88857F,new Date())).
                build());

        amqpChannel.send(
                MessageBuilder.withPayload(new Rate("JPY",102.17F,new Date())).
                build());

        amqpChannel.send(
                MessageBuilder.withPayload(new Rate("MXN",19.232F,new Date())).
                build());

        amqpChannel.send(
                MessageBuilder.withPayload(new Rate("GBP",0.75705F,new Date())).
                build());
    };
}
```

You can see from this snippet that we are using the amqpChannel and sending the Rate as a message. If you run it, take a look at your RabbitMQ Web Console and see the four messages in JSON format sitting in the spi.rate queue.

AMQP Consumer

If you need a consumer, you will use `inboundAdapter`. You can use the following code in the `RateConfig` class:

```
@Bean IntegrationFlow incomingRateFlow(
                ConnectionFactory connectionFactory,
                @Value("${apress.spi.queue}") String queue){
    return IntegrationFlows
      .from(Amqp.inboundAdapter(connectionFactory,queue)
          .messageConverter(new Jackson2JsonMessageConverter()))
      .handle("simpleMessageHandler","process")
      .get();
}
```

This code shows you the consumer, where the `Amqp.inboundAdapter` is used, by passing the `connectionFactory`, `queue`, the converter, and its handle by the `simpleMessageHandler` bean.

■ **Note** If you wondering about the `ConnectionFactory` reference, remember that Spring Boot will configure this automatically. If you want to connect to a remote server, just add the `spring.rabbitmq.*` properties in the `application.properties` file.

Currency Exchange Project

Based on what you learned in the previous sections, imagine that the currency exchange project will start receiving new rates through a file and then will send them to a RabbitMQ queue and to a processed file at the same time. How can you implement this feature? You need a way to send a message to two recipients.

Try to solve this issue without looking at the code. The `rest-api-si` project contains the solutions. You can see the code in the `RateSpiConfig` and the `RateServiceActivator` classes. A hint: I used the *recipient list* pattern. For writing out to a file, if I used the `Files.inboundAdapter`, what would I use for writing files out?

Summary

This chapter covered Enterprise Integration patterns and discussed how the Spring Integration module gives you all the necessary components to create enterprise-ready and integration solutions using Spring Boot.

It showed you the different ways of programming Spring Integration with Spring Boot. It also showed you how to combine XML, Java Config, and annotations to create an integrated application.

Why is Spring Integration important? The next chapter shows that the Spring Cloud Stream technology is based on Spring Integration and it's an even easier way to use all these components.

CHAPTER 9

■ ■ ■

Messaging with Spring Cloud Stream

So far you have seen all the messaging techniques that are available. Using the Spring Framework and Spring Boot makes it easy for developers and architects to create robust messaging solutions. This chapter takes a new step forward and enters into the new *Cloud Native Application Development*.

This chapter covers Spring Cloud Stream and how this new technology can help you write *message-driven microservices* applications.

Spring Cloud

Before I start talking about Spring Cloud Stream internals and usage, let's consider its umbrella project: *Spring Cloud*.

Spring Cloud is a set of tools that allows developers to create applications that use the common patterns in distributed systems, from configuration management, to service discovery, circuit breakers, smart routing, micro-proxy, control bus, global locks, distributed sessions, service-to-service calls, distributed messaging and much more. These distributed patterns are also covered in the microservices chapter.

Based on Spring Cloud, we have several projects, including Spring Cloud Config, Spring Cloud Netflix, Spring Cloud Bus, Spring Cloud for Cloud Foundry, Spring Cloud Cluster, Spring Cloud Stream, Spring Cloud Stream App Starters, and more.

If you want to start right away with any of these technologies, you need three things in your pom.xml file:

- Add the <parent/> tag with the spring-boot-starter-parent. For example:

```
<parent>
    <groupId>org.springframework.boot</groupId>
    <artifactId>spring-boot-starter-parent</artifactId>
    <version>1.4.4.RELEASE</version>
</parent>
```

© Felipe Gutierrez 2017

F. Gutierrez, *Spring Boot Messaging*, DOI 10.1007/978-1-4842-1224-0_9

- Add the `<dependencyManagement/>` tag with a GA release. For example:

```
<dependencyManagement>
    <dependencies>
        <dependency>
            <groupId>org.springframework.cloud</groupId>
            <artifactId>spring-cloud-dependencies</artifactId>
            <version>Camden.SR5</version>
            <type>pom</type>
            <scope>import</scope>
        </dependency>
    </dependencies>
</dependencyManagement>
```

- Add the technologies you want to use in the `<dependencies/>` tag. For example:

```
<dependencies>
 <dependency>
   <groupId>org.springframework.cloud</groupId>
   <artifactId>spring-cloud-starter-stream-rabbit</artifactId>
 </dependency>

 <!--MORE Technologies here -->

</dependencies>
```

If you take a deep look into the `pom.xml` file of a Spring Cloud annotation, you will see that the name convention is now `spring-cloud-starter-<technology to use>`. Also note that we added a dependency management tag that allows us to deal with all transitive dependencies and library version management.

Spring Cloud Stream

It's time to talk about Spring Cloud Stream. This is the focus here because we are talking about messaging in this book and also because Spring Cloud Stream is a lightweight messaging-driven microservices framework. It's based on Spring Integration and Spring Boot (providing the opinionated runtime for easy configuration), which means that you can create enterprise-ready messaging and integration solution applications with ease. It provides a simple declarative model for sending and receiving messages using either RabbitMQ or Apache Kafka.

I think one of the most important features of the Spring Cloud Stream is the decoupling of messaging between producers and consumers, by creating bindings that can be used out of the box. In other words, you don't need to add broker-specific code to your application for producing or consuming messages. You just add the required binding (I'll explain this later) dependencies to your application and Spring Cloud Stream will take care of the messaging connectivity and communication.

The next section describes the main components of the Spring Cloud Stream.

Spring Cloud Stream Concepts

Let's look at the main components of the Spring Cloud Stream:

- *Application model*: The application model is just a middleware-neutral core, which means that the application will communicate using input and output channels to external brokers (as a way of transporting messages) through binder implementations.

- *Binder abstraction*: Spring Cloud Stream provides at this moment the Kafka and RabbitMQ binder implementations. This abstraction makes it possible for Spring Cloud Stream apps to connect to the middleware. But, how does this abstraction know about the destinations? It can dynamically choose at runtime the destinations based on channels. Normally we need to provide this through the `application.properties` file as `spring.cloud.stream.bindings.[input|ouput].destination` properties.
  I'll discuss this when we look at the examples.

- *Persistent publish/subscribe*: The application communication will be through the well-known publish/subscribe model. If Kafka were used, it would follow its own topic/subscriber model, and if RabbitMQ were used, it would create a topic exchange and the necessary bindings for each queue. This model reduces any complexity of producer and consumer.

- *Consumer groups*: You will find out that your consumers will need to be able to scale up at some point. Scalability can be done using the concept of a consumer group (this is similar to the Kafka consumer groups feature), where you can have multiple consumers in a group for a load-balancing scenario. This makes the scale needs very easy to set up.

- *Partitioning support*: Spring Cloud Stream support data partition, which allows multiple producers to send data to multiple consumers and ensure that common data is processed by the same consumer instances. This is a benefit for performance and consistency of data.

- *Binder API*: Spring Cloud Stream provides an API interface. It's actually a binder SPI (Service Provider Interface) where you can extend the core by modifying the original code, so it's easy to implement a specific binder, such as JMS, WebSockets, etc.

This section covers about the programming model and the binders. If you want to know more about the other concepts, you can take a look at the Spring Cloud Stream reference. The idea is just to show you how to start creating event-driven microservices with Spring Cloud Stream. To show you what we are going to cover, take a look at Figure 9-1.

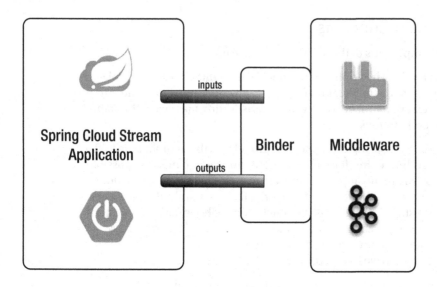

Figure 9-1. *Spring Cloud Stream application*

Spring Cloud Stream Programming

Following Figure 9-1, consider what would you need to create a Spring Cloud Stream app:

- `<dependencyManagement/>`: You need to add this tag with the latest Spring Cloud library dependencies.

- Binder: You need to choose what kind of a binder you will need:

  - Kafka: If you choose Kafka as your binder, you need to add the following dependency:

    ```
    <dependency>
        <groupId>org.springframework.cloud</groupId>
        <artifactId>spring-cloud-starter-stream-kafka</artifactId>
    </dependency>
    ```

  - RabbitMQ: If you choose RabbitMQ as your binder, you need to add the following dependency:

    ```
    <dependency>
        <groupId>org.springframework.cloud</groupId>
        <artifactId>spring-cloud-starter-stream-rabbit</artifactId>
    </dependency>
    ```

    You must also have Kafka or RabbitMQ up and running. You can even use both at the same time. You can configure them in the `application.properties` or `application.yml` files.

- @EnableBinding: This is a Spring Boot application, so just by adding @EnableBinding you can convert the app into a Spring Cloud Stream.

The following sections show you how to send and receive messages from one application to another using RabbitMQ as transport layer without knowing any specifics about the brokers API or how to configure the producer or consumer messages.

Spring Cloud Stream uses channels (input/output) as a mechanism to send and receive messages. A Spring Cloud Stream application can have any number of channels, and it defines two annotations: @Input and @Output. These annotations help to identify consumers from producers. Normally a SubscribableChannel class will be marked with @Input annotation and a MessageChannel class will be marked with @Output. They listen for incoming messages and send outgoing messages, respectively.

The SubscribableChannel and MessageChannel interfaces should be well known to you from the Spring Integration chapter. Remember that I told you that Spring Cloud Stream is based on Spring Integration.

If you don't want to deal directly with these channels and annotations, Spring Cloud Stream simplifies this by adding three interfaces that cover the most common messaging use cases: source, processor, and sink. Behind the scenes, these interfaces have the right channels (input/output) your application needs:

- *Source*: A source is used in an application where you are ingesting data from an external system (by listening into a queue, a REST call, file system, database query, etc.) and sending it through an output channel. This is the actual interface from Spring Cloud Stream:

```
public interface Source {

  String OUTPUT = "output";

  @Output(Source.OUTPUT)
  MessageChannel output();

}
```

- *Processor*: You can use a processor in an application when you want to start listening from the input channel for new incoming messages, process the message received (enhancements, transformations, etc.), and send a new message to the output channel. This is the actual interface from Spring Cloud Stream:

```
public interface Processor extends Source, Sink {

}
```

- *Sink*: You can use a sink application when you want to start listening from the input channel for new incoming messages, do some processing, and then end the flow (saving data, firing a task, logging into the console, etc.). This is the actual interface from Spring Cloud Stream:

```java
public interface Sink {

    String INPUT = "input";

    @Input(Sink.INPUT)
    SubscribableChannel input();

}
```

Figures 9-2 and 9-3 show the models we are going to start working on.

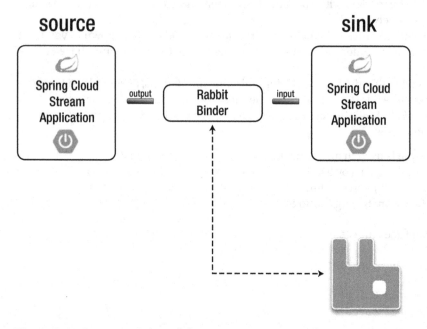

Figure 9-2. *Source to sink model*

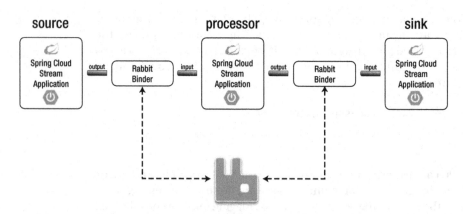

Figure 9-3. *Source to processor to sink model*

You can get all the examples from the book's source code. This chapter includes several examples. Let's get started and see some code.

cloud-stream-demo

The purpose of this project is to show how to create a source and send a message through its output channel, a processor, and how to receive and send messages from the input and output channels, respectively. You'll also create a sink and learn how to receive messages from the input channel. Practically, I'm showing what Figure 9-3 illustrates, but considering each Stream app one at a time.

Right now the communication between these application is manual, meaning that we need to do some steps in between, and this is because I want you to learn how each of these applications works. In the next section, you are going to see how the whole flow works.

Source

We are going to start by defining a source. Remember that this component has an output channel. Open the `com.apress.messaging.cloud.stream.SimpleSource` class. It should look like Listing 9-1.

Listing 9-1. com.apress.messaging.cloud.stream.SimpleSource.java

```
@EnableBinding(Source.class)
public class SimpleSource {

    private SimpleDateFormat simpleDate =
                        new SimpleDateFormat("HH:mm:ss");


    @Bean
    @InboundChannelAdapter(channel=Source.OUTPUT)
    public MessageSource<String> simpleText(){

        return () -> MessageBuilder
                .withPayload("Hello at " +
                    simpleDate.format(new Date()))
                .build();
    }
}
```

Listing 9-1 shows you the simplest Source stream application you can have. Let's take a look:

- @EnableBinding: This annotation will enable this class as a Spring Cloud Stream application, and it will enable the necessary configuration for sending or receiving messages through the provided binder.

- Source: This interface marks the Spring Cloud Stream app as a source stream. It will create the necessary channels; in this case the output channel that will be used to send messages to the provided binder.

- @InboundChannelAdapter: This annotation is part of the Spring Integration framework. It simply polls over the simpleText method every second. This means that a new message will be sent every second. You can change the frequency and the number of messages by adding a poller and modifying the default settings. For example:

  ```
  @InboundChannelAdapter(value = Source.OUTPUT, poller = @Poller
  (fixedDelay = "5000", maxMessagesPerPoll = "3"))
  ```

  The important part of this declaration is the channel, where in this case it's pointing to Source.OUTPUT. This means that it will use the output channel (MessageChannel output()).

- MessageSource: This is an interface that sends a Message<T>, which is a wrapper that has payload and headers.

- MessageBuilder: You are already familiar with this class, which sends a MessageSource type. In this case, we are sending "Hello at - Date" as a string message.

Before you run the example, make sure you have RabbitMQ up and running. Next, run the example. You might not see too much, but there is something going on behind the scenes. Follow these steps:

1. Open RabbitMQ Web Management in a browser. Go to http://localhost:15672. The username and password are guest. Go to the Exchanges tab, as shown in Figure 9-4.

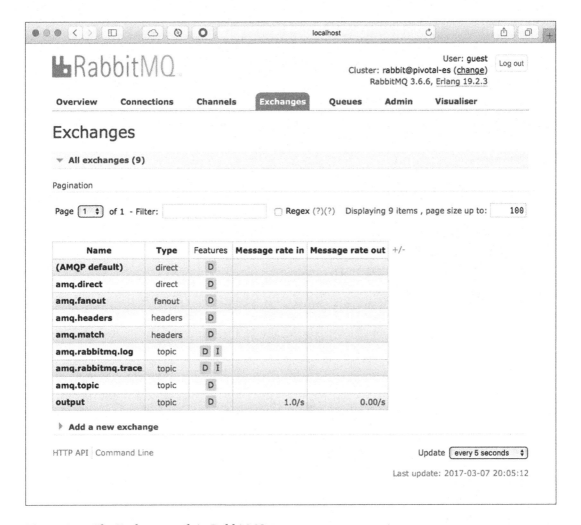

Figure 9-4. *The Exchanges tab in RabbitMQ*

Note that an output (a topic exchange) was created and the message rate is 1.0/s.

2. Next, you'll create a queue so you can bind this exchange to it. Go to the Queues tab and create a new queue named my-queue. See Figure 9-5.

***Figure 9-5.** The Queues tab of RabbitMQ*

3. Once the queue is created, it appears in the list. Next, click the my-queue queue, go to the Bindings section, and add the binding. See Figure 9-6 for the proper values.

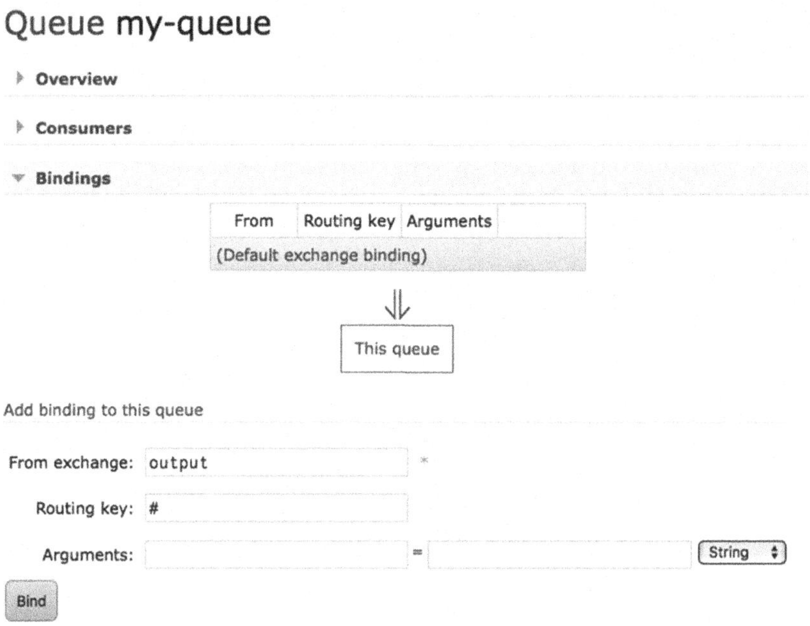

Queue my-queue

▶ **Overview**

▶ **Consumers**

▼ **Bindings**

From	Routing key	Arguments
(Default exchange binding)		

⇓

This queue

Add binding to this queue

From exchange: `output`   *

Routing key: `#`

Arguments: [   ] = [   ] [String ◆]

[Bind]

Figure 9-6. *The Bindings tab of RabbitMQ*

Fill out the From Exchange field with the value output (this is the name of the exchange) and the Routing Key field with the value #. This will allow any message to get into the my-queue queue.

4. A few seconds after you bind the output exchange to the my-queue queue, you will start seeing several messages. Open the Overview panel shown in Figure 9-7.

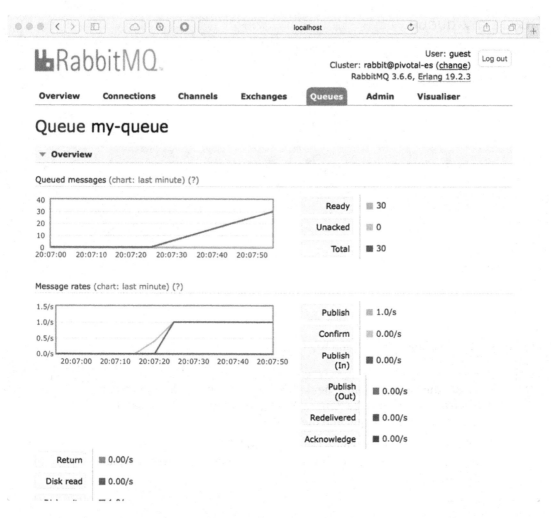

Figure 9-7. *The Overview tab of RabbitMQ*

5.   Let's review a message by opening the Get Messages panel. You can get any number of messages and view their contents. See Figure 9-8.

Figure 9-8. *Getting messages from RabbitMQ*

After you choose several messages, take a look at the payload. You will have a message every second. Note also that the message has properties, such as the headers with the contentType: text/plain and the delivery_mode: 2 (this means the messages are being persisted). This is how Spring Cloud Stream and its binder connect to RabbitMQ to publish messages.

Processor

This example uses a listener for the channel input (where all incoming messages arrive). It will get a string message and will convert it to uppercase, then it will send the string to the output channel.

Open the com.apress.messaging.cloud.stream.SimpleProcessor class. It should look like Listing 9-2.

Listing 9-2. com.apress.messaging.cloud.stream.SimpleProcessor.java

```
@EnableBinding(Processor.class)
public class SimpleProcessor {

    @StreamListener(Processor.INPUT)
    @SendTo(Processor.OUTPUT)
    public String transformToUpperCase(String message) {
        return message.toUpperCase();
    }
}
```

Listing 9-2 shows you a simple processor stream. Let's review it:

- @EnableBinding: This annotation will enable this class as a Spring Cloud Stream application, and it will enable the necessary configuration for sending or receiving messages through the provided binder.

- Processor: This interface marks the Spring Cloud Stream app as a processor stream. It will create the necessary channels. In this case, it creates the input channel (for listening for new incoming messages) and output channel (for sending messages to the provided binder).

- @StreamListener: This annotation is part of the Spring Cloud Stream framework and it's very similar to @RabbitListener and @JmsListener. It will listen for new incoming messages in the Processor.INPUT channel (SubscribableChannel input()).

- @SendTo: You already know this annotation; it's the same one we used in previous chapters. Its task is the same and you can see it as a reply or just as a producer. It will send a message to the Processor.OUTPUT channel (MessageChannel output()).

This is a trivial, but good, example of what you can do with a processor stream. Before you run it, make sure to comment out the @EnableBinding annotation from the SimpleSource class and to delete the output exchange and the my-queue queue.

Run the example. Again, the application is not doing too much, but let's go to the RabbitMQ Web Management.

1. Go to your browser and visit the http://localhost:15672 site (username and password are guest). Click on the Exchanges tab, and you will see the same output exchange and a new input exchange being created. Remember that the processor stream will use the input and output channels. See Figure 9-9.

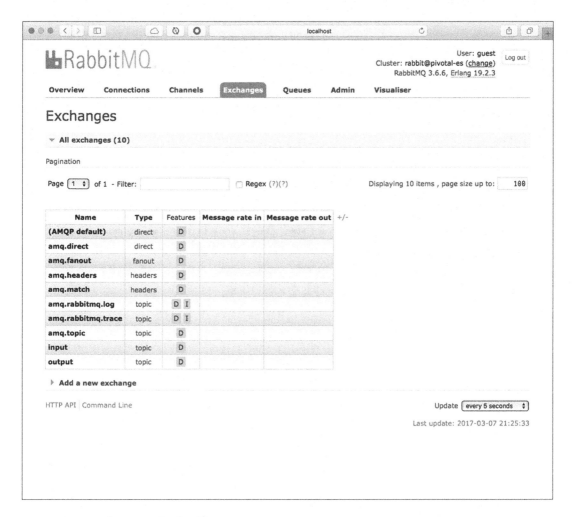

Figure 9-9. *Exchanges tab of RabbitMQ*

Note that there is no longer any message rates in any of the new exchanges.

2. Next, go to the Queues tab. Notice that a new queue was created, called `input.anonymous`, and it includes random text. See Figure 9-10.

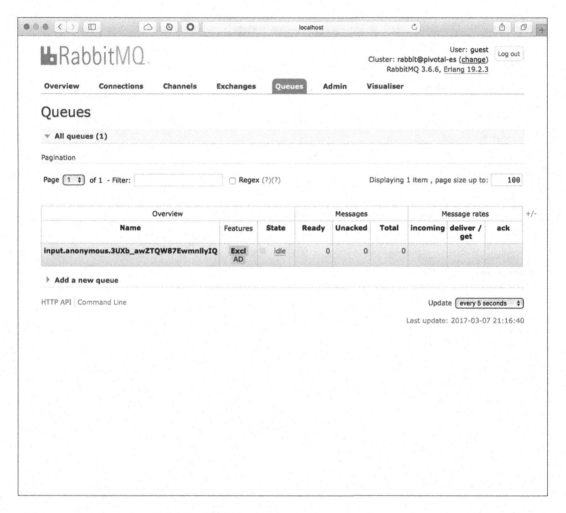

Figure 9-10. *The Queues tab of RabbitMQ*

Practically that's it; the SimpleProcessor stream created the output exchange and the input.anonymous.* queue, which means that the stream is connected to the binder, in this case RabbitMQ. So you might wonder how to send a message. There are different ways to do it, and one is to emulate a message using the RabbitMQ. You can also send them programmatically. The following sections show both methods.

We are going to create a queue named my-queue and bind it to the output, which is very similar to what you did in the source stream example.

1. Go to the Queues tab and create a queue named my-queue. Bind it to the output exchange with a routing key #. This is similar to Steps 2 and 3 from the source stream. Note that input.anonymous.* queue has a binding to the input exchange.

2. Now we are going to send a message using the `input` exchange. Go to the Exchanges tab and click on the `input` exchange. Select the Publish Message panel. Add to the Payload field this text: `this is just a test`. See Figure 9-11.

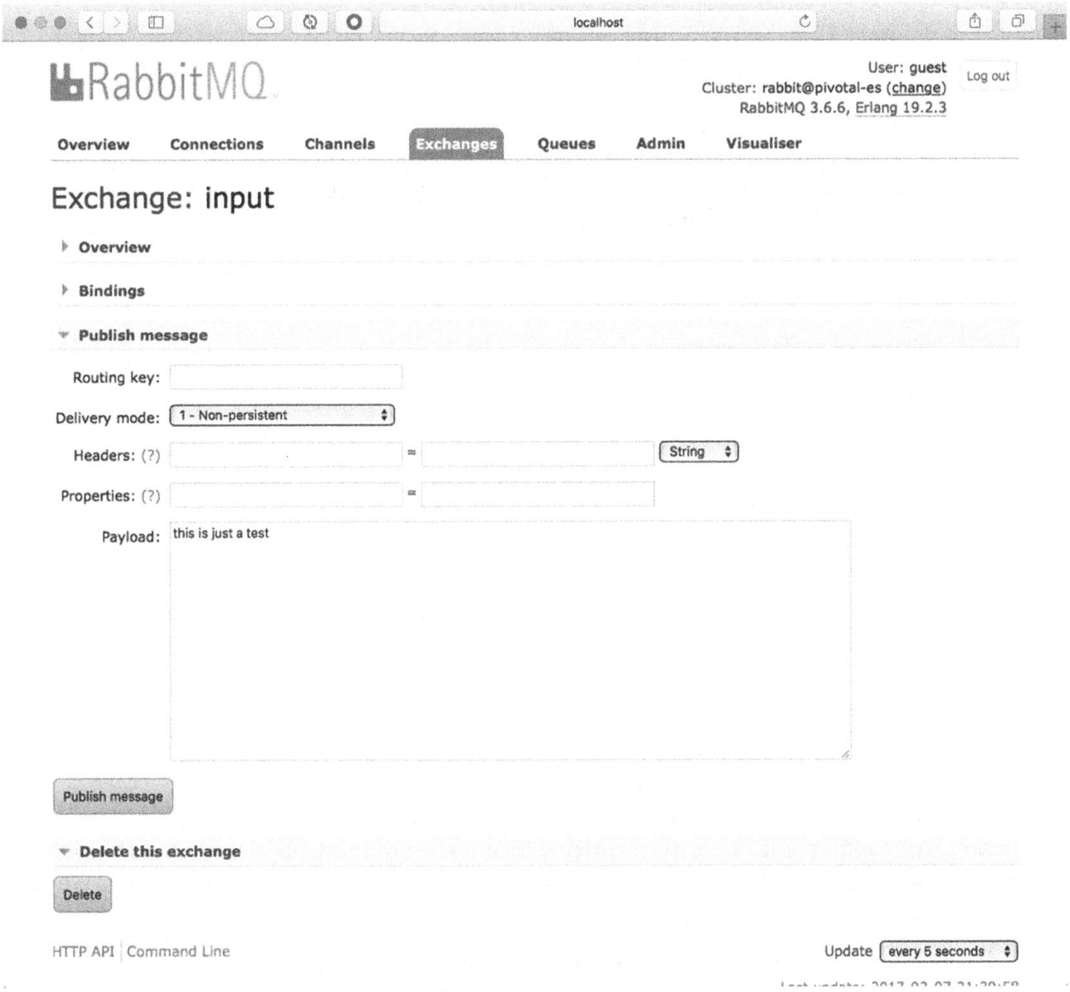

Figure 9-11. *Publishing a message from RabbitMQ*

Then click the Publish Message button. A message saying `Message Published` should appear.

3. Next, take a look at the logs. You should see something similar to what's shown in Figure 9-12.

```
2017-03-07 21:42:57.712  INFO 35332 --- [KWiQMceWqIDsQ-1] c.apress.messaging.aop.CloudStreamAudit  :
=====================================
[BEFORE]
 Class: com.apress.messaging.cloud.stream.SimpleProcessor$$EnhancerBySpringCGLIB$$d9872ad2
Method: transformToUpperCase
Params:
> arg0: 116,104,105,115,32,105,115,32,106,117,115,116,32,97,32,116,101,115,116

[AFTER]
Return: 116,104,105,115,32,105,115,32,106,117,115,116,32,97,32,116,101,115,116
=====================================
```

Figure 9-12. *Application logs*

> If you look at the my-queue queue and get the message, you should have practically the same result. See Figure 9-13.

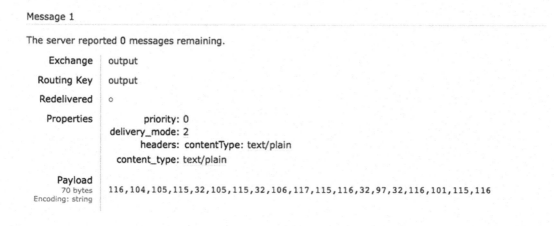

Figure 9-13. *Getting the messages from RabbitMQ*

Wait a minute! It seems that we are getting some array, which is not being converted to uppercase. If you analyze the code, those are ASCII codes, yet nothing happens. This is because the input channel receives the text that was converted (by RabbitMQ) as an array of bytes. We can fix this.

4. Before we fix this, purge the queue of messages by clicking the Purge button at the end of the queue page. You now start with an empty queue.

5. Go back to the Input exchange. Now we are going to pass the header that has content_type: text/plain, so that RabbitMQ doesn't change it to a byte array. See Figure 9-14.

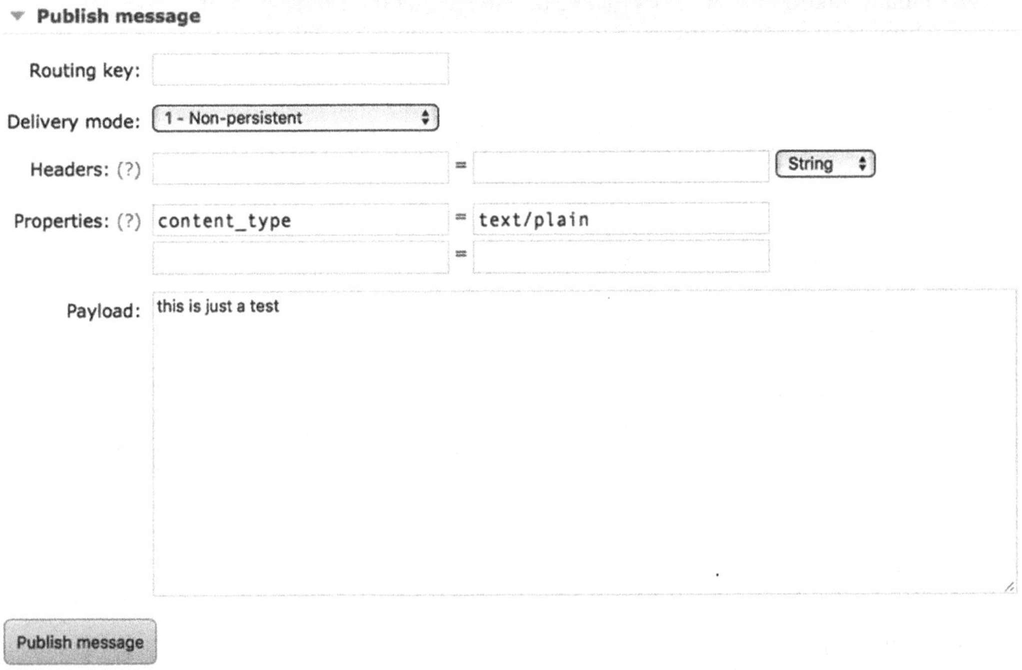

▼ **Publish message**

Routing key:

Delivery mode: [1 - Non-persistent ⬍]

Headers: (?) [ ] = [ ] [String ⬍]

Properties: (?) `content_type` = `text/plain`

[ ] = [ ]

Payload: this is just a test

[Publish message]

Figure 9-14. *Changing to text/plain in RabbitMQ*

Publish the message and take a look at the logs. The processor now
returns THIS IS JUST A TEST.

6. Finally, take a look at the my-queue queue and get the message. You should see the text converted to uppercase, as shown in Figure 9-15.

Message 1

The server reported 0 messages remaining.

Exchange	output
Routing Key	output
Redelivered	○
Properties	priority: 0 delivery_mode: 2 headers: contentType: text/plain content_type: text/plain
Payload 19 bytes Encoding: string	THIS IS JUST A TEST

Figure 9-15. The text is now uppercase

What would happen if you wanted to set another content type, like a Java object, JSON object, or XML object? It would be a hassle to modify this at the RabbitMQ level. There should be another way, and there is! This is just an example of trying to send a message and see the behavior of the processor stream; in real life you would never use RabbitMQ like this. You would use it only to monitor message rates, but that's it.

So, in order to use a content type, you must add a property to the application.properties (or application.yml) file that allows you to convert any message to the type specified. In this case, you use the following property:

```
spring.cloud.stream.bindings.input.content-type=text/plain
```

The key here is the input property. Note that we pass the content-type. If you do the change and restart the app, you can now send a message (in lowercase) without any header or property and you should have the text in uppercase (in the logs and in the my-queue queue).

I mentioned that you can send messages programmatically. You can do that by adding this functionality to your main class. See Listing 9-3.

Listing 9-3. com.apress.messaging.CloudStreamDemoApplication.java

```
@SpringBootApplication
public class CloudStreamDemoApplication {

    public static void main(String[] args) {
        SpringApplication.run(
                    CloudStreamDemoApplication.class, args);
    }
```

```
    @Bean
    CommandLineRunner sourceSender(MessageChannel input){
        return args ->{
            input
            .send(MessageBuilder
                    .withPayload("hello world")
            .build());
        };
    }
}
```

If you run the application, HELLO WORLD in uppercase appears in the logs and in the my-queue queue. As you can see, we are using a method that you already know from the Spring Integration, the MessageChannel interface. What is interesting here is that Spring knows what channel to inject. Remember that the @Processor annotation exposes the input channel.

Sink

The Sink stream will create an input channel to listen for new incoming messages. Open the com.apress.messaging.cloud.stream.SimpleSink class. See Listing 9-4.

Listing 9-4. com.apress.messaging.cloud.stream.SimpleSink.java

```
@EnableBinding(Sink.class)
public class SimpleSink {

    @StreamListener(Sink.INPUT)
    public void process(String message){

    }

}
```

Listing 9-4 shows you a Sink stream, and you already know about the annotations. The @EnableBinding will convert this class to a Source stream and it will listen for new incoming message through @StreamListener and the Sink.INPUT channel. The Sink.INPUT will create an input channel (SubscribableChannel input()).

If you use the same Listing 9-3 and run the application, take a look at the RabbitMQ management. You will see the input exchange and the input.anonymous.* bound to each other. At the log levels, should you have something similar to Figure 9-16.

```
2017-03-07 22:33:37.798  INFO 39620 --- [ restartedMain] c.apress.messaging.aop.CloudStreamAudit  :
====================================
[BEFORE]
 Class: com.apress.messaging.cloud.stream.SimpleSink$$EnhancerBySpringCGLIB$$927cdaaa
Method: process
Params:
> arg0: hello world

[AFTER]
Return: void/null
====================================
```

Figure 9-16. *Application logs*

Remember, the Sink stream will do some extra work with the message it received, but it will end the flow.

What I explained so far doesn't do too much, because I wanted you to understand how this works internally first. Now, let's consider a real-life scenario, where we actually create a complete flow and see how the streams communicate with each other without going into the RabbitMQ management.

Microservices

Even though there is a chapter dedicated to microservices, this section touches on this new way to create scalable and highly available applications using this new concept. The most important part is to be able to communicate between streams using messaging. You should consider each stream (each source, processor, and sink) as a microservice.

Example Features

This list includes some of the features (requirements) needed for this example. This is a complete flow that will allow us to print movie tickets. Here are the requirements:

- All persons are received in CSV format in the contacts.txt file.

- Each person includes first name, last name, date of birth, phone, e-mail, and friend fields. The Friend field is a Boolean that indicates if this is a friend or not.

- After reading the contacts.txt file, the example must process each person and then create a movie ticket using the following rules:

  - If the person is a friend, he or she gets free popcorn.

  - If the person is a friend, the movie is free; otherwise, the cost is $15.75.

  - Set an expiration date for the movie tickets. They are valid for a week.

- Movie tickets must be sent to a queue in JSON format, so it's easy for other clients to read them.

- *Optional.* Create a queue for friends and non-friends.

For this flow, I created three separate projects: cloud-stream-source-demo, cloud-stream-processor-demo, and cloud-stream-sink-demo. Each one needs to run separate and must start in the following order: sink, processor, and last source.

The next sections explain the main code of these three projects.

cloud-stream-source-demo

Open the com.apress.messaging.cloud.stream.PersonFileSource class. See Listing 9-5.

Listing 9-5. com.apress.messaging.cloud.stream.PersonFileSource.java

```
@EnableBinding(Source.class)
public class PersonFileSource {

    private PersonFileProperties props;
    private PersonConverter personConverter;

    public PersonFileSource(
                    PersonFileProperties props,
                    PersonConverter personConverter){
        this.props = props;
        this.personConverter = personConverter;
    }

    @Bean
    public IntegrationFlow fileFlow(){
        return IntegrationFlows
            .from(Files.inboundAdapter(
                    new File(this.props.getDirectory())))
                    .preventDuplicates(true)
                .patternFilter(this.props.getNamePattern()),
                e -> e.poller(Pollers.fixedDelay(5000L)))
                .split(Files.splitter().markers())
            .filter(p -> !(p instanceof FileSplitter.FileMarker))
            .transform(Transformers.converter(personConverter))
            .channel(Source.OUTPUT)
            .get();
    }
}
```

Listing 9-5 shows the source stream. Note that it uses the IntegrationFlow class to create the File reading, a small transformation into a Person object. It's then sent to the Source.OUTPUT channel.

Next, open application.properties. See Listing 9-6.

Listing 9-6. src/main/resources/application.properties

```
server.port=${port:8081}
```

spring.cloud.stream.bindings.output.destination=person

```
apress.stream.file.directory=.
apress.stream.file.name-pattern=*.txt
```

Listing 9-6 shows you the application.properties file. As you can see, it start in port 8081 if the port argument is not specified at runtime. What is important here is the output.destination allows us to create a channel named person. Why is this necessary? Remember that the streams (source, processor, and sink) use the same name of the channels. If we don't change the destination, no files will be processed. If we start with the source, the source needs to send to the output, but the processor also has an output, so which channel will be used? There is a conflict here. That's why we need to add the destination. Once you run this example, it will become clear.

cloud-stream-processor-demo

Open the com.apress.messaging.cloud.stream.PersonTicketProcessor class. See Listing 9-7.

Listing 9-7. com.apress.messaging.cloud.stream.PersonTicket.java

```
@EnableBinding(Processor.class)
public class PersonTicketProcessor {

    private List<String> movieTitles =
                Arrays.asList("Dead Pool 2"
                                ,"The Incredibles 2"
                                ,"Avatar 2","Tarzan 2"
                                ,"Cars 3");
        private Random rand = new Random();

    @StreamListener(Processor.INPUT)
    @SendTo(Processor.OUTPUT)
    public Ticket process(Person person) {
        Ticket ticket = new Ticket();
        ticket.setPerson(person);
        ticket.setMovieTitle(
                    movieTitles.get(
                    rand.nextInt(movieTitles.size())));
        ticket.setFreePopcorn(person.isFriend());
        ticket.setCost(person.isFriend() ? 0.0f: 15.75f);
        ticket.setValidUntil(
                new DateTime(new Date()).plusWeeks(1).toDate());

        return ticket;
    }

}
```

Listing 9-7 shows you the processor stream. As you can see, nothing is new. We are receiving a person, but we are returning a ticket, and of course we are doing the logic based on the requirements.

Next, open the application.properties file. See Listing 9-8.

Listing 9-8. src/main/resources/application.properties

```
server.port=${port:8082}
```

spring.cloud.stream.bindings.input.destination=person
spring.cloud.stream.bindings.output.destination=tickets

spring.cloud.stream.bindings.output.content-type=application/json

spring.jackson.date-format=yyyy-MM-dd

Listing 9-8 shows the application.properties file. Remember that the processor stream has input and output channels, so we need to rename them by adding the destination to each one. The input channel will be named person and the output will be named tickets.

Recall that one of the requirements is to have the ticket in JSON format, which is why we add the content-type as application/json. This will convert the ticket using the Jackson library into JSON format. Finally, we add a better date format.

cloud-stream-sink-demo

Open the com.apress.messaging.cloud.stream.TicketSink class. See Listing 9-9.

Listing 9-9. com.apress.messaging.cloud.stream.TicketSink.java

```
@EnableBinding(Sink.class)
public class TicketSink {

    @Bean
    public IntegrationFlow toAmqp(
            RabbitTemplate rabbitTemplate,
            @Value("${ticket.exchange:}") String exchange,
            @Value("${ticket.queue}") String queue){
                return IntegrationFlows
                        .from(Sink.INPUT)
                        .handle(
                            Amqp
                            .outboundAdapter(rabbitTemplate)
                            .exchangeName(exchange)
                            .routingKey(queue))
                        .get();
    }
```

```
    @Bean
    public Queue rateQueue(
                        @Value("${ticket.queue}") String queue){
        return new Queue(queue,true);
    }
}
```

Listing 9-9 shows you the Sink source. You know all the code, as it uses the @ EnableBinding(Sink.class) to make a Spring Cloud Stream app that will create an input channel to receive a message. It also uses the IntegrationFlow class, which will send the incoming message to the specified queue.

Next, open the application.properties file. See Listing 9-10.

Listing 9-10. src/main/resources/application.properties

```
server.port=${port:8083}
```

spring.cloud.stream.bindings.input.destination=tickets

ticket.queue=processed.tickets

Listing 9-10 shows you the application.properties file. Again, the input channel will be renamed tickets, and the queue is named processed.tickets, where the Sink stream will send the JSON message. Before you run each project, look at Figure 9-17.

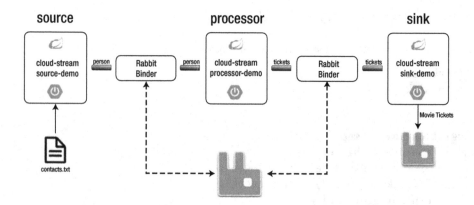

Figure 9-17. *Example flow*

Figure 9-17 shows you the whole configuration. Notice why we need to change the channel names. I provided a small contacts.txt file in the source stream, so you should good to go. If you are using STS IDE, try to run it in this order: sink, processor, source. This is because you want to make sure the processor and sink are listening. Once they run, you should have the exchanges and queues created, as well as the messages. See Figures 9-18 (for the exchanges), 9-19 (for the queues), and 9-20 (for the ticket).

Exchanges

▼ All exchanges (10)

Pagination

Page [1 ▼] of 1 - Filter: [   ] ☐ Regex (?)(?)

Name	Type	Features	Message rate in	Message rate out	+/-
(AMQP default)	direct	D	0.00/s	0.00/s	
amq.direct	direct	D			
amq.fanout	fanout	D			
amq.headers	headers	D			
amq.match	headers	D			
amq.rabbitmq.log	topic	D I			
amq.rabbitmq.trace	topic	D I			
amq.topic	topic	D			
person	topic	D	0.00/s	0.00/s	
tickets	topic	D	0.00/s	0.00/s	

Figure 9-18. *Exchanges (person, tickets)*

Queues

▼ All queues (3)

Pagination

Page [1 ▼] of 1 - Filter: [   ] ☐ Regex (?)(?)   Displaying 3 items , page size up to: [100]

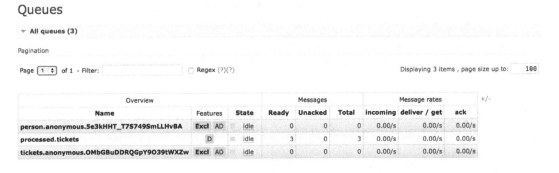

Overview				Messages			Message rates			+/-
Name	Features	State	Ready	Unacked	Total	incoming	deliver / get	ack		
person.anonymous.5e3kHHT_T7S749SmLLHvBA	Excl AD	idle	0	0	0	0.00/s	0.00/s	0.00/s		
processed.tickets	D	idle	3	0	3	0.00/s	0.00/s	0.00/s		
tickets.anonymous.OMbGBuDDRQGpY9O39tWXZw	Excl AD	idle	0	0	0	0.00/s	0.00/s	0.00/s		

Figure 9-19. *Queues (person, tickets, and processed.tickets)*

Message 1

The server reported 2 messages remaining.

Exchange	(AMQP default)
Routing Key	processed.tickets
Redelivered	○
Properties	priority: 0 delivery_mode: 2 headers: contentType: application/json;charset=UTF-8 content_encoding: UTF-8 content_type: application/json;charset=UTF-8
Payload 254 bytes Encoding: string	{"id":"deb20bb6-cc0c-4034-b1fc-595bebbcc958","person":{"first":"John","last":"Doe","dob":"2000-01-22","phone":"+1 345-834-6789","emai

Figure 9-20. *The processed.tickets message*

Congratulations! You created a data-driven microservices solution with Spring Cloud Stream. Imagine what you can do with this technology.

Before we continue, did you realize that we are missing an optional feature—a dynamic routing? Don't worry, you will create it in the currency project!

Spring Cloud Stream App Starters

What about if I tell you that we could avoid creating the previous example and just use the Spring Cloud Stream app starters?

The Spring Cloud Stream provides out-of-the-box applications starters that run. The Spring Cloud team already implemented around 52 applications that you can just download, configure, and execute. These application starters are divided by source, processor, and sink model:

- *Source*: file, ftp, gemfire, gemfire-cq, http, jdbc, jms, load-generator, loggregator, mail, mongodb, rabbit, s3, sftp, syslog, tcp, tcp-client, time, trigger, triggertask, and twitterstream

- *Processor*: bridge, filter, groovy-filter, groovy-transform, httpclient, pmml, scriptable-transform, splitter, tcp-client, and transform

- *Sink*: aggregate-counter, cassandra, counter, field-value-counter, file, ftp, gemfire, gpfdist, hdfs, hdfs-dataset, jdbc, log, rabbit, redis-pubsub, router, s3, sftp, task-launcher-local, task-launcher-yarn, tcp, throughput, and websocket

So, let's create an example using the `source:http` and the `sink:log`. I added the necessary JARs in this chapter in the folder `ch09/app-starters`. You will find a subfolder for each JAR and a `start.sh` script.

source:http

Open a terminal and execute the `start.sh` script from the `http` subfolder. Or you can execute the following command:

```
java -jar http-source-rabbit-1.1.2.RELEASE.jar --spring.cloud.stream.bindings.
output.destination=simple-demo
```

Note that we are passing some arguments about the destination. Of course, you can create an `application.properties` file and put it into the same directory with this property. The `source:http` JAR will run in the 8080 port.

sink:log

Open a new terminal and execute the `start.sh` script from the `log` subfolder. Or you can execute the following command:

```
java -jar log-sink-rabbit-1.1.1.RELEASE.jar --spring.cloud.stream.bindings.input.
destination=simple-demo --server.port=8081
```

Note that we are passing the same arguments as the source:http, but in this case for the input channel and it's running in the 8081 port.

Now you are ready to test. Use the cURL command to post a message (Windows users can use POSTMAN(https://www.getpostman.com/). For example:

```
$ curl -X POST -d "Hello Spring Cloud Starter Apps" localhost:8080
```

The sink:log log prints out a byte array, right? Try this new command:

```
$ curl -X POST -d "Hello Spring Cloud Starter Apps" localhost:8080 -H "Content-Type: text/plain"
```

You should get the message Hello Spring Cloud Starter Apps. See Figure 9-21.

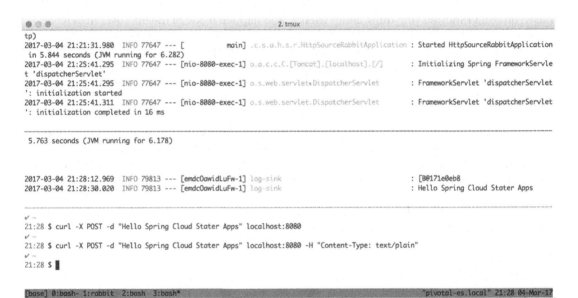

Figure 9-21. *source:http | sink:log*

▪ **Note**   You can get the latest release of the app starters at http://repo.spring.io/libs-release/org/springframework/cloud/stream/app/.

If you want to use the other Spring Cloud Stream Application Starters and see their configurations, you can take a look at http://docs.spring.io/spring-cloud-stream-app-starters/docs/Avogadro.SR1/reference/html/ for reference.

Currency Project

For the currency project, imagine you will get several rates from a source and, based on the rate's code, you need to send this rate to the right consumer. In other words, if you send a rate from JPY, it will choose the destination JPY to send it. This is similar to the dynamic routing that you want to have for the microservices example.

Take a look in the `rest-api-cloud-stream` project, the `com.apress.messaging.cloud.stream.RateProcessor` class for a dynamic routing. Also look at the `com.apress.messaging.RestApiCloudStreamApplication` class (the main class), as it has a new way to send messages using the Source stream.

What's Next?

Based on what I showed you, think about what would happen if one of the microservices went down. Would your entire flow be down? How can you solve the point of failure and add high availability? How can you orchestrate all these microservices? How can you avoid zero downtime?

The good thing is that Spring Cloud Stream is the base of Spring Cloud Data Flow technology. Spring Cloud Data Flow is an orchestration service for composable microservice applications that live in a cloud environment, and it is very useful for real-time data analytics and Big Data solutions.

The benefit of using Spring Cloud Data Flow is that this technology is supported by Cloud Foundry, Apache Mesos, Kubernetes, and Apache Yarn. Spring Cloud Data Flow relies on these technologies to orchestrate register, creation, deployment, and tasks over a cloud infrastructure, plus it's compatible with Spring Cloud Services (something that I'll talk in the microservices chapter).

The recommendation here is to look at this awesome technology. You will be confortable learning that, because it's all about Spring Cloud Stream.

Summary

This chapter showed you how easy you can create simple Stream applications with Spring Cloud Stream and Spring Boot. Simply by using the `@EnableBinding` annotation and the binder, you can create message-driven solutions.

I also showed you that Spring Cloud Stream has application starters that can be used just by adding the appropriate configuration.

The next chapter discusses a new trending technology, reactive frameworks. In this case, we cover the Spring Reactor project for creating non-blocking applications on the JVM based on the Reactive Stream specification.

CHAPTER 10

■ ■ ■

Reactive Messaging

Nowadays the practice of being *reactive* is at the top of all IT companies' goals. There are also related terms that we are hearing often, such as *reactive programming, functional reactive programming,* and *reactive streams.* Even though there are different, what we are seeing here is a change to how we are tackling data consumption, concurrency, asynchronous events, high performance, and distributed computing.

This chapter discusses reactive programming and messaging. This is not a new topic. Several years ago, Microsoft released the C# Reactive extensions (in a formal way) and JavaScript was gaining momentum in being reactive to events. Not only that, this concept has been around since the 60s, when programmers wanted to interconnect hardware.

Let's start by learning more about reactive programming and what is good for. Later, you learn what kind of frameworks will help you with this new micro-event reactive architecture.

Reactive Programming

Reactive programming is a way to deal asynchronously with event data streams (in a non-blocking form) that change over time. It's a way to react to their changing behavior.

Reactive programming is good for the following use cases:

- *Spreadsheets/cells*: When you open your spreadsheet application, have you imagined how it works internally? Every cell can have other cell dependencies, so any new change in one needs to be reflected in the others—this is being reactive to change. Also imagine your matrix when you are doing Calculus or Algebra computations. How can you react to a value in a particular matrix cell? Normally, you start dealing with event-driven architectures.

- *High concurrent messaging*: Messaging in my opinion is the most critical part of every system. The idea of sending a few thousand or even millions of messages per second has been always the goal. Being able to process all these messages and consume them concurrently (synchronously and asynchronously) has also been a challenge.

- *External service calls*: Nowadays devices (cell phones, tablets, sensors, etc.) require a lot of information with a single swipe, gesture, or click. Their backend services need to collect data from different services (local or remote) and aggregate information into a single response. They become very chatty and sometimes very slow. Reactive programing is a good fit here.

© Felipe Gutierrez 2017
F. Gutierrez, *Spring Boot Messaging*, DOI 10.1007/978-1-4842-1224-0_10

- *Async processing*: This has been a dangerous territory for many developers, because every time we start thinking about async processes, we need to think about threads, callbacks, concurrency, orchestration, and more. With reactive programming, we are almost there.

Most of the solutions to these use cases involve creating libraries with non-blocking I/O, like event-machine (from the Ruby programming language), which worked and performed very well.

Java and its new `java.util.concurrent` package expose the Future/CompletableFuture interfaces. *Map-Reduce* and *Fork-Join* help in parallel processing with Big Data scenarios. *Actor Models* expose concurrency in a natural way, one of the important implementations is in the Akka framework.

Reactive programming is the next step in creating a system that is responsive, resilient, elastic, and of course message-driven in a asynchronous way, allowing flow control and applying back-pressure when necessary. All of these features are provided with non-blocking communication. In contrast with Java 8 streams or Iterable/Iterator, which are just pull-based, reactive programming is push-based. In other words, reactive programming deals with synchronous/pull and asynchronous/push concepts.

It's time to focus on the implementation. The following sections use two main modules or libraries: RxJava and Reactor. Then we cover the new upcoming release of Spring Framework 5 and its WebFlux module.

■ **Note** This chapter contains five projects that we are going to use in the following sections: `rxjava-demo`, `reactor-demo`, `web-emitter`, `spring-web-flux`, and `spring-web-flux-reactive`.

RxJava

RxJava came from Netflix (called ReactiveX; see `http://reactivex.io`) and is a library for composing asynchronous and event-based programs by using observable sequences. It extends the observer pattern and supports sequences of data. It removes the complexity of threading, synchronization, thread safety, concurrent data structures, and non-blocking I/O by providing a simple API.

RxJava provides a collection of operators that can filter, select, transform, combine, and compose observables, allowing for a better and more efficient execution and composition. It exposes several classes like `Observable`, which we are going to see in the example code.

The rxjava-demo Project

Open the `com.apress.messaging.RxJavaDemoApplication` class. See Listing 10-1.

Listing 10-1. com.apress.messaging.RxJavaDemoApplication.java

```
@SpringBootApplication
public class RxJavaDemoApplication {

    private static final Logger log =
            LoggerFactory.getLogger(RxJavaDemoApplication.class);
```

```
public static void main(String[] args){
  log.info("Demo Steam Application");
  new SpringApplicationBuilder(RxJavaDemoApplication.class)
            .web(false)
            .run(args);
}

@Bean
CommandLineRunner rxJava(ExchangeService service){
    return args -> {
        log.info("RxJava >> Observable");
        Observable<Exchange> exchange =
                            service.getExchangeRates();
        exchange.subscribe(System.out::println);

};
}
```

Listing 10-1 shows you the main application where a basic Observable instance is being defined:

- Observable<Exchange>: Here we are using the Observable class that supports not just the emission of single scalar values (like Java 8 Future), but also supports sequences of values or even infinite streams. In this case, it supports an Exchange class that contains the rates.

- subscribe: The Observable class has some similarities to its Java cousin Iterable (normally doing a pull when invoking the next() method over it). In this case, we are going to do a push, by calling subscribe. This subscriber will receive all the messages (the exchange rates) and print them out.

The Observable type adds something that's missing from the observer pattern: the ability for the producer to tell the consumer that there is no more data available by signaling the observer (subscriber) using the onCompleted method, and the ability for the producer to let know the consumer that there has been an error, by signaling the observer (subscriber) using the onError method.

Next, let's see an Observable that will push data on to the subscriber. Open the com.apress. messaging.service.ExchangeService class. See Listing 10-2.

Listing 10-2. com.apress.messaging.service.ExchangeService.java

```
@Service
public class ExchangeService {
    private static final Logger log =
                LoggerFactory.getLogger(ExchangeService.class);
    private Exchange exchange;

    ExchangeService() {
        SortedMap<String, Float> rates =
                                new TreeMap<String, Float>() {
```

```
                {
                        put("EUR", 0.942013F);
                        put("JPY", 114.75440909F);
                        put("MXN", 19.598225F);
                        put("GPB", 0.819626F);
                }
        };
        exchange = new Exchange(rates, new Date());
    }

    public Observable<Exchange> getExchangeRates() {
        return Observable.unsafeCreate(subscriber -> {

        while(!subscriber.isUnsubscribed()) {

            try {
                Float factor =
                    (new Random().nextFloat() * 2 - 1) / 10F;
                subscriber.onNext(
                    new Exchange(exchange
                            .getRates()
                            .entrySet()
                            .stream()
                            .collect(
                                Collectors.toMap(
                                        entry ->
                                        entry.getKey(),

        entry -> entry.getValue()
                    * factor + entry.getValue(),
        (v1, v2) -> {
                    throw new RuntimeException(String.format("Duplicate key for
                    values %s
                    and %s", v1, v2));
                                                }, TreeMap::new)), new Date())));

            if (new Random().nextInt(100) > 90 )
                throw new Exception(
                        "Some values are getting too high!!");
            sleep(1000);

        } catch (Exception ex){
          log.error(ex.getMessage());
        }
      }
    });

  }
```

```
private void sleep(int ms) {
    try {
    Thread.sleep(ms);
    } catch (Exception ex) {}
}

}
```

Listing 10-2 shows you the service. The observable will push an exchange rate every second. Take a moment to analyze the code, and then we can analyze it together:

- Observable.unsafeCreate: This will return an observable that executes the given OnSubscribe action for each Subscriber (see Listing 10-1). With this observable, you can execute onError(Throwable) when an error occurs or onCompleted() when there is no more data. One of the important parts here is subscriber.isUnsubscribee() in the while statement. Here we are determining whether we have more subscribers. We are going to see this in the next examples.

- subscriber.onNext: This provides the observer (subscriber) with a new item (the exchange rate) to the observer. This method call is pushing the values to the subscriber. See Listing 10-1.

This particular service will send an exchange rate every second (see the sleep statement). The exchange rate varies because a factor is applied to it to emulate real scenarios in the money exchange world.

If you run the application, you should get something similar to Figure 10-1.

```
2017-03-17 14:22:24.697  INFO 15094 --- [ restartedMain] c.a.messaging.RxJavaDemoApplication    : RxJava >> Observable
Exchange [base=USD, rates={EUR=0.9106505, GPB=0.7923381, JPY=110.93388, MXN=18.94574}, timestamp=Fri Mar 17 14:22:24 MDT 2017]
Exchange [base=USD, rates={EUR=0.8767704, GPB=0.7628597, JPY=106.80666, MXN=18.240875}, timestamp=Fri Mar 17 14:22:25 MDT 2017]
Exchange [base=USD, rates={EUR=0.8981804, GPB=0.7814882, JPY=109.4148, MXN=18.686304}, timestamp=Fri Mar 17 14:22:26 MDT 2017]
Exchange [base=USD, rates={EUR=1.0064027, GPB=0.87565005, JPY=122.59825, MXN=20.937828}, timestamp=Fri Mar 17 14:22:27 MDT 2017]
Exchange [base=USD, rates={EUR=0.885202, GPB=0.77019584, JPY=107.833786, MXN=18.416292}, timestamp=Fri Mar 17 14:22:28 MDT 2017]
```

Figure 10-1. *Application logs*

Figure 10-1 shows you the logs of your first reactive application. Next, let's modify the main class and add a subscriber implementation. See Listing 10-3.

Listing 10-3. com.apress.messaging.RxJavaDemoApplication.java

```
@SpringBootApplication
public class RxJavaDemoApplication {

    private static final Logger log =
        LoggerFactory.getLogger(RxJavaDemoApplication.class);
```

```java
public static void main(String[] args){
  log.info("Demo Steam Application");
  new SpringApplicationBuilder(RxJavaDemoApplication.class)

        .web(false)
        .run(args);

}

@Bean
CommandLineRunner rxJava(ExchangeService service){
    return args -> {

    Observable<Exchange> observableExchange =
                                service.getExchangeRates();
     observableExchange.subscribe(new Subscriber<Exchange>(){

        @Override
        public void onCompleted() {
            log.info("EXCHANGE COMPLETED!!");
        }

        @Override
        public void onError(Throwable t) {
            log.error("EXCHANGE IS SKYROCKETING... >> " +
                                    t.getMessage());
            unsubscribe();
        }

        @Override
        public void onNext(Exchange ex) {
            log.info(ex.toString());

            if(ex.getRates().get("JPY").floatValue() >
                                            125.0F){
                log.warn(">>> JPY rate is now to high: " +
                ex.getRates().get("JPY")
                .floatValue() + ", is time to quit. Bye.");
                unsubscribe();
            }
        }
    });

    };
  }
}
```

Listing 10-3 shows you a more complete example. In this case, we are not just doing reference methods (System.out::println), but are creating a new Subscriber<Exchange> and overriding some methods:

- Subscriber<Exchange>: This is an abstract class that provides a way to receive
  push-based notifications from Observables and permits manual unsubscribing from these Observables.

- onError: This method notifies the observer that the Observable has an error condition.

- onCompleted: This method notifies the observer that the Observable has finished sending push-based notifications.

- onNext: This method provides to the observer with a new item (in this case, a new exchange rate) to observe. Note in this method that there is an unsubscribe() call that will set the flag so the Observable in the subscriber.isUnsubscribed() evaluates to true and will end the while statement.

If you run the application, you should see something similar to Figure 10-2.

```
: Exchange [base=USD, rates={EUR=0.8872843, GPB=0.77200764, JPY=108.08745, MXN=18.459614}, timest
: Exchange [base=USD, rates={EUR=0.91583717, GPB=0.7968509, JPY=111.56571, MXN=19.053646}, timest
: Exchange [base=USD, rates={EUR=0.9623452, GPB=0.8373166, JPY=117.23124, MXN=20.021227}, timesta
: Exchange [base=USD, rates={EUR=1.0186327, GPB=0.88629115, JPY=124.08809, MXN=21.192268}, timest
: Exchange [base=USD, rates={EUR=0.93019104, GPB=0.8093399, JPY=113.31427, MXN=19.352272}, timest
: Exchange [base=USD, rates={EUR=0.9462369, GPB=0.8233011, JPY=115.26896, MXN=19.686102}, timesta
: Exchange [base=USD, rates={EUR=0.9940623, GPB=0.864913, JPY=121.09496, MXN=20.68109}, timestamp
: Exchange [base=USD, rates={EUR=1.026297, GPB=0.89295965, JPY=125.02173, MXN=21.351719}, timesta
: >>> JPY rate is now to high: 125.02173, is time to quit. Bye.
: Some values are getting too high!!
: Started RxJavaDemoApplication in 8.235 seconds (JVM running for 8.833)
: Closing org.springframework.context.annotation.AnnotationConfigApplicationContext@2e7f9748: sta
: Unregistering JMX-exposed beans on shutdown
```

Figure 10-2. *Logs*

Figure 10-2 shows the logs after running the application. Note that the JPY rate triggered the unsubscribe() call, which means the Observable will stop sending push-based exchange rates.

Note that I included more code in the book's source that I don't cover here, and I want you to experiment with it. Take a moment to analyze what is going on. I added an example on how to interact with a fixed number of push-based exchange rates.

So far these examples are running in the same main thread, but there is a way to use multithreading. Take at look at code where you can use your own thread pool with an ExecutorService class. For example:

```
ExecutorService executorService =
                        Executors.newFixedThreadPool(100);

Observable<Exchange> observableExchange =
                        service.getExchangeRates();
```

```
observableExchange
    .take(10)
    .subscribeOn(
            Schedulers
                .from(executorService))
                .forEach(ex -> { log.info(ex.toString()); });
```

RxJava right now is up to version 2.x and it changed some of the signatures. You can check for changes at https://github.com/ReactiveX/RxJava/wiki/What's-different-in-2.0.

Reactor

Reactor (from the Spring Framework team) is a fully mature and non-blocking reactive programming foundation for the JVM. It plays along with all the Java 8 functional APIs (*CompletableFuture, Stream,* and *Duration*), offers two composable asynchronous sequences APIs (*Flux*—N elements and *Mono*—0 or 1 elements), and implements the Reactive Extension specifications.

You can get more information about Reactor at http://projectreactor.io/. Let's start with the code.

The reactor-demo Project

This project is very similar to what we saw with RxJava, but this time, instead of Observable, we are going to see Flux. Open the com.apress.messaging.ReactorDemoApplication class. See Listing 10-4.

Listing 10-4. com.apress.messaging.ReactorDemoApplication.java

```
@SpringBootApplication
public class ReactorDemoApplication {

    private static final Logger log =
            LoggerFactory
                    .getLogger(ReactorDemoApplication.class);

    public static void main(String[] args) throws IOException {
        SpringApplication.run
                    (ReactorDemoApplication.class, args);
        System.in.read();
    }

    @Bean
    CommandLineRunner reactorFlux(ExchangeService service){
        return args -> {
```

```
        log.info("Reactor >> Flux");
        Flux<Exchange> fluxExchange =
                        service.getExchangeRates();
        fluxExchange.subscribe( ex -> log.info(ex.toString()));
    }
  }
}
```

Listing 10-4 shows you the Reactor way, using Flux and the subscribe method call for push-based data streams. Flux represents a reactive sequence of *0..N* items (in this case, the exchange rates).

Behind the scenes, Flux is described as Flux<T> and implements a Publisher<T> interface. This interface is a provider of a unbounded number of sequenced elements, and it publishes them according to the demand from its subscribers. A publisher can serve multiple subscribers (Subscriber<T> interface) in a dynamically way at various points in time.

Let's take a look at the service. Open the com.apress.messaging.service.ExchangeService class. See Listing 10-5.

Listing 10-5. com.apress.messaging.service.ExchangeService.java

```
@Service
public class ExchangeService {
    private static final Logger log =
                LoggerFactory.getLogger(ExchangeService.class);
    private Exchange exchange;

    ExchangeService() {
        log.info(">>> Exchange Service created.");
        @SuppressWarnings({ "serial" })
        SortedMap<String, Float> rates =
                    new TreeMap<String, Float>() {
                    {
                            put("EUR", 0.942013F);
                            put("JPY", 114.75440909F);
                            put("MXN", 19.598225F);
                            put("GPB", 0.819626F);
                    }
                };
        exchange = new Exchange(rates, new Date());
    }

    public Flux<Exchange> getExchangeRates(){
        return Flux.create( sink -> {
            while(true){
                Float factor =
                        (new Random().nextFloat() * 2 - 1) / 10F;
```

171

```
            sink.next(
                    new Exchange(
                    exchange
                        .getRates()
                        .entrySet()
                        .stream()
                        .collect(
                                Collectors.toMap(

entry -> entry.getKey(),
entry -> entry.getValue() * factor + entry.getValue(),
 (v1, v2) -> {
        throw new RuntimeException(
String.format("Duplicate key for values %s and %s", v1, v2));
            }, TreeMap::new)), new Date()));

            sleep(1000);

            if(factor > 0.095F)
                    sink.complete();
            }
        });
    }

    private void sleep(int ms) {
        try {
            Thread.sleep(ms);
        } catch (Exception ex) { }
    }
}
```

Listing 10-5 shows you Subscriber using Flux<Exchange> by calling the create method. This method receives a Consumer<? Super FluxSink<T>>. This consumer is just a simple call that needs to be executed. The parameter needs to be a FluxSink<T> type interface. This interface is a wrapper API around a downstream subscriber and sends any number of signals followed by zero or at least one onError or onComplete.

If you run the application, you should see something similar to Figure 10-3.

```
: Registering beans for JMX exposure on startup
: Reactor >> Flux
: Exchange [base=USD, rates={EUR=0.9849666, GPB=0.8569989, JPY=119.98693, MXN=20.491856}, timest
: Exchange [base=USD, rates={EUR=0.90861076, GPB=0.79056334, JPY=110.6854, MXN=18.903303}, times
: Exchange [base=USD, rates={EUR=0.8533833, GPB=0.7425111, JPY=103.95769, MXN=17.754316}, timest
: Exchange [base=USD, rates={EUR=0.9848913, GPB=0.8569334, JPY=119.97776, MXN=20.49029}, timesta
```

Figure 10-3. Logs

What is the difference between using RxJava and Reactor? Reactor supports functional programming, schedulers, low latency, and the Lambda pipeline approach. One of the greatest benefits of Reactor is that it supports all the HTTP MVC types from Spring, which is a streaming functionality (Server Sent Events—SSE) out of the box.

I added more examples to the project. You just need to enable them and then run, experiment, and play with them.

Spring 5: WebFlux Framework

Spring 5 has many of new features, including support for JDK 9. One of its major features is the *Functional Web Framework* or *WebFlux,* which is based on Reactor.

The Servlet 3.1 specification was capable of non-blocking I/O, but not as well as you might think. The rest of the Servlet API is still an imperative style and can't be used in a reactive, non-blocking stack.

The Spring team includes the `spring-webflux` module to add a new functional programming model to web applications. Together with `spring-mvc`, you can have a reactive stack web framework. The `spring-webflux` module also has a reactive `WebClient` that is a non-blocking alternative to the `RestTemplate` class, which allows you to deal with asynchronous and streaming scenarios. See Figure 10-4.

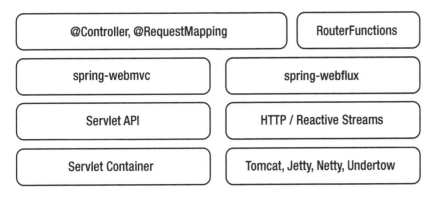

Figure 10-4. Spring WebFlux

Programming Models

Spring WebFlux has two programming models: *annotation-based* and *functional-based.*

Annotation-Based Programming Model

You can use the same well-known annotations from the `spring-webmvc` module; the main difference is that the core is now non-blocking and operates on the reactive `ServerHttpRequest` and `ServerHttpResponse` responses (instead of the `HttpServletRequest` and `HttpServletResponse` responses).

Open the `spring-web-flux-reactive` project and then open the `com.apress.messaging.controller.ReactiveController` class. See Listing 10-6.

Listing 10-6. com.apress.messaging.controller.ReactiveController.java

```java
@RestController
public class ReactiveController {

    SubscribableChannel personChannel;
    PersonRepository repo;

    public ReactiveController(SubscribableChannel
                personChannel, PersonRepository repo){
                this.personChannel = personChannel;
                this.repo = repo;
    }

    @GetMapping("/person")
    Flux<Person> list() {
        return Flux.fromStream(this.repo.getAll());
    }

    @GetMapping("/person/{id}")
    Mono<Person> findById(@PathVariable String id) {
        return Mono.just(this.repo.findOne(id));
    }

    @GetMapping(value="/person-watcher",
                produces=MediaType.TEXT_EVENT_STREAM_VALUE)
    public Flux<Person> log4Person(){
        return Flux.create( sink -> {
                MessageHandler handler = message ->
                sink.next((Person) message.getPayload());
                    personChannel.subscribe(handler);
                  sink.setCancellation(() ->
                  personChannel.unsubscribe(handler));
                  });

    }

    @PostMapping(value="/person", consumes =
                    {MediaType.APPLICATION_JSON_VALUE})
    public void createPerson(@RequestBody Person person){
        if(person != null && person.getName() != null){
            repo.save(person);
            personChannel
        .send(MessageBuilder.withPayload(person).build());
        }
    }

}
```

Listing 10-6 shows you the annotation you have seen from Spring MVC, but now they are based on Reactive streams. Analyze the code and note that we are using the Reactor programming model—the Flux and Mono reactive classes.

Even though I am not going to talk in detail about the Server Sent Events (SSE) technology, spring-webflux brings this technology just by producing the TEXT_EVENT_STREAM_VALUE content-type. The SSE is a way to send messages from the server to a web page (via push notifications).

■ **Note**   The web-emitter project contains an example of an SSE. SSE was included in Spring 4.2, so this is not a new technology. It's been around a couple of years. The browsers are the ones that need to implement the way to receive notifications.

Functional-Based Programming Model

You can use functional programming to configure all the requests and responses from the server. You define RouterFunctions, HandlerFunctions, and a server.

RouterFunctions, HandlerFunctions, and Server

Spring WebFlux includes several reactive classes and concepts that make it even easier to model the web requests and responses:

- HandlerFunctions: All the requests are handled by a HandlerFunction<T>, which takes the ServerRequest and returns a Mono<ServerResponse>.

- RouterFunctions: All the incoming requests are routed to handler functions with a RouterFunction<T>, which takes a ServerRequest and returns a Mono<HandlerFunction> type.

- Server: A new server needs to be configured in order to take the new RouterFunctions and Handlers.

The spring-web-flux project contains all the code you are going to need in this section.

Start by opening the configuration that contains all the RouterFunctions. Open the com.apress.messaging.config.ServerConfig class. See Listing 10-7.

Listing 10-7. com.apress.messaging.config.ServerConfig.java

```java
@Configuration
public class ServerConfig {

    PersonHandler handler;
    ServerConfig(PersonHandler handler){
        this.handler = handler;
    }
```

```
@Bean
RouterFunction<ServerResponse> router(){
    return RouterFunctions
    .route(GET("/persons/{id}")
        .and(accept(APPLICATION_JSON)), handler::findById)
    .andRoute(GET("/persons")
        .and(accept(APPLICATION_JSON)), handler::findAll)
    .andRoute(GET("/personwatcher")
        .and(accept(APPLICATION_JSON)),
                                    handler::newPersonLog)
    .andRoute(POST("/persons")
    .and(accept(APPLICATION_JSON)), handler::createPerson);
}


@Bean
HttpServer httpServer(
                    RouterFunction<ServerResponse> router){
    HttpHandler httpHandler =
                    RouterFunctions.toHttpHandler(router);
    ReactorHttpHandlerAdapter adapter = new
                    ReactorHttpHandlerAdapter(httpHandler);
    HttpServer server =
                    HttpServer.create("localhost", 8080);
    server.newHandler(adapter).block();
    return server;
    }
}
```

Listing 10-7 shows you the functional programming required to configure the new reactive web stack, by creating the RouterFunctions. You can think of it as a new way to create web controllers. Note that we are defining routes and handlers.

Listing 10-7 shows you how to configure a server. In this example, the Netty server is being configured. Note how HttpHandler and ReactorHttpHandler are being used.

Next, open the com.apress.messaging.handler.PersonHandler class. See Listing 10-8.

Listing 10-8. com.apress.messaging.handler.PersonHandler.java

```
@Component
public class PersonHandler {
    PersonRepository repo;
    EmitterProcessor<Person> stream =
        EmitterProcessor.<Person>create().connect();

    PersonHandler(PersonRepository repo) {
        this.repo = repo;
    }
```

```java
public Mono<ServerResponse>
                    findAll(ServerRequest request) {
    Flux<Person> people =
                        Flux.fromStream(this.repo.getAll());
    return
            ServerResponse
            .ok()
            .contentType(APPLICATION_JSON)
            .body(people, Person.class);
}


public Mono<ServerResponse>
                    findById(ServerRequest request) {
    String personId = request.pathVariable("id");
    Mono<ServerResponse> notFound =
                            ServerResponse.notFound().build();
    Mono<Person> personMono =
                Mono.just(this.repo.findOne(personId));

    return personMono
            .then(person ->
                    ServerResponse
                    .ok()
                    .contentType(APPLICATION_JSON)
                    .body(fromObject(person)))
            .otherwiseIfEmpty(notFound);
}


public Mono<ServerResponse>
                    createPerson(ServerRequest request) {
    Mono<Person> person =
                    request.bodyToMono(Person.class);
    return ServerResponse
            .ok()
            .build(person.doOnNext(p -> {
                this.repo.save(p);
                this.stream.onNext(p);
            }).then());
}

public Mono<ServerResponse>
                    newPersonLog(ServerRequest request){
    Mono<Person> personMono = stream.doOnNext( person -> {
    System.out.println(">>>> [Person created] " + person);
    })
                    .next()
                    .subscribe();
```

177

```
        personMono.block();
        return personMono
                    .then(person ->
                    ServerResponse
                    .ok()
                    .contentType(APPLICATION_JSON)
                    .body(fromObject(person)));
    }
}
```

Listing 10-8 shows the handler that will be used for each router function. Note that every method receives the ServerRequest as a parameter and returns a Mono<ServerResponse>.

■ **Note**   To run the spring-web-flux-reactive and spring-web-flux projects, you need to have the Mongo server up and running.

Summary

This chapter introduced reactive programming, including discussing what it's good for and what we can do with it. There is a lot of reactive programming right now and a lot to explain, and this chapter is just a start.

You saw two modules/libraries—RxJava (from Netflix) and Reactor (from the Spring Framework team). You also saw a sneak peek of what is coming in a few weeks with Spring 5 and the Functional Web: WebFlux.

In the next chapter, we are going to talk about microservices and you'll learn how you can apply all that you have learned so far in the book to your microservices-based projects.

## CHAPTER 11

Microservices

This chapter discusses the Microservices architecture and covers the changes that you need to make in order to get into a cloud-native application design using microservices. It also covers how messaging is an important key for success.

What Microservices Are

Microservices are not new; they have been around since the creation of UNIX. UNIX has many small programs (called commands) that do various tasks and can communicate with each other to create even better solutions. How do they do this?

If you are an experienced UNIX programmer, you already know the answer. The way these commands communicate is through pipes, |, which allow UNIX to pass information to the next available program or command. For example:

```
ls -al | grep Aug | grep -v '200[456]' | more
```

If you now start thinking about your own systems and applications, how can you do the same? Can you create small domain-based applications that communicate with other applications?

Microservices have gained a lot of enthusiasm among architects, developers and ops teams, but why do we need them? I think time is an essential part of the puzzle, because applications need to be fast, resilient, highly available, and scalable, all the while with high performance.

- *Speed*: You need to deliver faster than your competitors. You can use microservices that help you deliver faster in time-to-market scenarios.

- *Safety*: You need to maintain stability, availability, and durability in whole development cycle, through monitoring, isolation, tolerance, and auto-recovery practices. Start thinking about continuing delivery and integration.

- *Scalability*: Vertical scaling (that is, buying more hardware) doesn't scale well. Use commodity hardware, reuse what you have and scale horizontally, and create multiple instances of the same application. Use containers to help you scale.

- *Mobility*: Prepare to support multiple devices, from any location at any time. Mobile devices connect to the Internet, not only for social media, emails, and chats, but also for monitoring houses, engines, and more.

© Felipe Gutierrez 2017

F. Gutierrez, *Spring Boot Messaging*, DOI 10.1007/978-1-4842-1224-0_11

Everything seems to make sense, right? But I haven't explained how a microservice can communicate with multiple other microservices. Messaging is the key! Many companies use RESTful APIs to communicate with other systems or programs, even legacy systems, by creating decorators, translators or facades, but you have more options for communication, including HTTP, TCP (Web Socket, AMQP), Reactive Streams, and more.

The basic guides for creating microservices in a simple way are called the twelve-factor app principles.

The Twelve Factor Apps

To outline what you need to create a cloud-native architecture, the engineers at Heroku (see https://www.heroku.com/) have identified patterns that have become the twelve-factor application guide (see https://12factor.net/). This guide shows you how an application (a single unit) needs to be architected. It focuses on declarative configuration, being stateless, and being deployment independent. In other words, your applications need to be fast, safe, and scalable.

Here's a summary of the twelve-factor application guide:

- *Codebase*: One codebase tracked in VCS, many deploys. One app has a single codebase and it's tracked by a version control system like Git, Subversion, Mercurial, etc. You can do many deployments (from the same codebase) to the development, testing, staging, and production environments.

- *Dependencies*: Explicitly declare and isolate dependencies. Sometimes your environments won't have Internet connections (if it's a private system), so you need to think about packaging your dependencies (jars, gems, shared libraries, etc.). If you have an internal repository of libraries, you can declare manifest-like poms, gemfiles, bundles, etc. Never assume that you will have everything in your final environment.

- *Configuration*: Store the config in the environment. You shouldn't hardcode anything that varies. Use the environment variables or a configuration server.

- *Backing services*: Treat backing services as attached resources. Connect to services via URLs or the configuration.

- *Build, release, run*: Strictly separate build and run stages. Related to CI/CD (Continuous Integration, Continuous Delivery).

- *Processes*: Execute the app as one or more stateless processes. Processes should not store internal states. Share nothing. Any necessary state should be considered a *backing service*.

- *Port binding*: Export services via port binding. Your application is a self-container, and these apps are exposed via port binding. An application can become another app service.

- *Concurrency*: Scale out via the process model. Scale by adding more application instances. Individual processes are free to multithread.

- *Disposability*: Maximize robustness with fast startup and graceful shutdown. Processes should be disposable (remember they are stateless) and fault tolerant.

- *Environment parity*: Keep the development, staging, and production environments as similar as possible. In other words, take a look at the OS you install, and the frameworks, runtimes, or libraries versions you use. They must be the same on each environment. This is a result of high quality and ensures continuous delivery.

- *Logs*: Treat logs as event streams. Your apps should write to stdout. Logs are streams of aggregated, time-ordered events.

- *Admin processes*: Run admin and management tasks as one-off processes. Run admin processes on the platform: DB migrations, one-time scripts, etc.

Some programmers think that you need to have a cloud infrastructure in place to use microservices, but in my opinion, you don't need this. If you follow these principles, you will be ready to compete with bigger companies. When you are ready to move or switch to a better infrastructure, you are already there.

If you want to start creating microservices and follow these twelve-factor principles, it's not enough for a single or small team to create everything from scratch. You'll face several changes:

- *Cultural*: We need to move away from people silos and start creating cross-functional teams. They work better and are dedicated to solving one-domain business scenarios. Start thinking about continuous delivery, decentralize the decision-making, and look for team autonomy.

- *Organizational*: Create business capability teams that are cross-functional. These teams have autonomy to make their own decisions. Create the platform team operations, which should also be cross-functional.

- *Technical*: Get away from building monolith apps and get into microservice architectures. Think about bounded contexts. Follow some of the principles and practices of domain-driven design. Start by using containerization, to gain the isolation, scalability, and high performance of your app, then look for service integrations that give you control over distribution. See Figure 11-1.

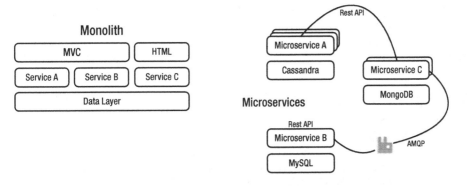

Figure 11-1. *Monolith approach versus using microservices*

Spring Cloud Services

Spring Cloud Services are a set of tools/frameworks that develops microservice architectures easily, quickly, and safely. This section covers the most common Spring Cloud services: Spring Cloud Config, Service Registry, and Circuit Breaker.

Spring Cloud Config Server

The Config Server is an externalized application configuration service that gives you a central place to manage your application's external properties across environments. See Figure 11-2.

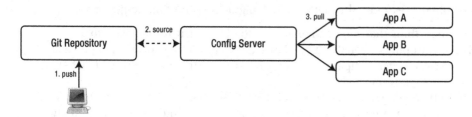

Figure 11-2. *Config Server*

You can use the Config Server during the development phase or with your pipeline (continuous delivery). You can manage every environment in a centralized way to access the common external configuration, without repackaging or redeploying.

Cloud Config Server

To use the Config Server, this is what you need to do:

1. In your pom.xml file, you need to use the following <dependency/> and the <dependencyManagement/> tags:

```
...
<dependency>
    <groupId>org.springframework.cloud</groupId>
    <artifactId>spring-cloud-config-server</artifactId>
</dependency>
...

<dependencyManagement>
    <dependencies>
        <dependency>
            <groupId>org.springframework.cloud</groupId>
            <artifactId>spring-cloud-dependencies</artifactId>
            <version>Camden.SR6</version>
            <type>pom</type>
```

```
        <scope>import</scope>
      </dependency>
    </dependencies>
  </dependencyManagement>
</dependencyManagement>
```

At the time of this book writing, the version was Camdem.SR6. To keep updated, take a look at the main web project found at `http://projects.spring.io/spring-cloud/`.

2. Add `@EnableConfigServer`:

```
@SpringBootApplication
@EnableConfigServer
public class ConfigServerDemoApplication {

    public static void main(String[] args) {
        SpringApplication.run(
                ConfigServerDemoApplication.class, args);
    }
}
```

`@EnableConfigServer` will create the Config Server that will get the latest values from GitHub and process the request from the clients.

3. Add the `application.properties` (or `application.yml`) file where the Git repository is located by providing the URI.

```
# Default port
server.port=8888

# Spring Config Server
spring.cloud.config.server.git.uri=https://github.com/<github-username>
/your-repo-app-config.git
```

That's it; you don't need anything else. You can now run the Config Server. You can take a look at the `config-server-demo` project.

Cloud Config Client

To connect to the Cloud Config Server, you need to do the following:

1. Add the `<dependency/>` and the `<dependencyManagement/>` tags to your `pom.xml` file:

```
...
<dependency>
    <groupId>org.springframework.cloud</groupId>
    <artifactId>spring-cloud-starter-config</artifactId>
</dependency>
```

```
...
<dependencyManagement>
    <dependencies>
        <dependency>
            <groupId>org.springframework.cloud</groupId>
            <artifactId>spring-cloud-dependencies</artifactId>
            <version>Camden.SR6</version>
            <type>pom</type>
            <scope>import</scope>
        </dependency>
    </dependencies>
</dependencyManagement>
```

That's it. You can now use any property like you are used to doing, either using a regular @Value("${hello-world-message}") or via @ConfigurationProperties. You can get a complete example in the config-client-demo project.

I think this is very straightforward solution. If you need more in-depth references, visit the http://projects.spring.io/spring-cloud/ web site.

Service Registry

The Service Registry provides the implementation of the *Service Discovery pattern*. This pattern is one of the most important features of the microservice architecture. See Figure 11-3.

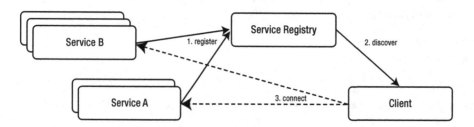

Figure 11-3. *Service Registry*

When a client registers to the Service Registry, it provides metadata about itself like its host and port number. It also keeps sending heartbeats to the Service Registry. The Service Registry has everything in memory.

Service Registry: Eureka Server

In order to use the Service Registry (the Eureka server), you need to do the following:

1. Add the <dependency/> and the <dependencyManagement/> tags to your pom.xml file:

```
<dependency>
    <groupId>org.springframework.cloud</groupId>
    <artifactId>spring-cloud-starter-eureka-server</artifactId>
</dependency>
...
<dependencyManagement>
    <dependencies>
        <dependency>
            <groupId>org.springframework.cloud</groupId>
            <artifactId>spring-cloud-dependencies</artifactId>
            <version>Camden.SR6</version>
            <type>pom</type>
            <scope>import</scope>
        </dependency>
    </dependencies>
</dependencyManagement>
```

2. Add @EnableEurekaServer to your application:

```
@SpringBootApplication
@EnableEurekaServer
public class ServiceRegistryDemoApplication {

    public static void main(String[] args) {
        SpringApplication.run(
                ServiceRegistryDemoApplication.class, args);
    }
}
```

@EnableEurekaServer calls up a web page. You can look at
http://localhost:8761/ in your browser, as shown in Figure 11-4.

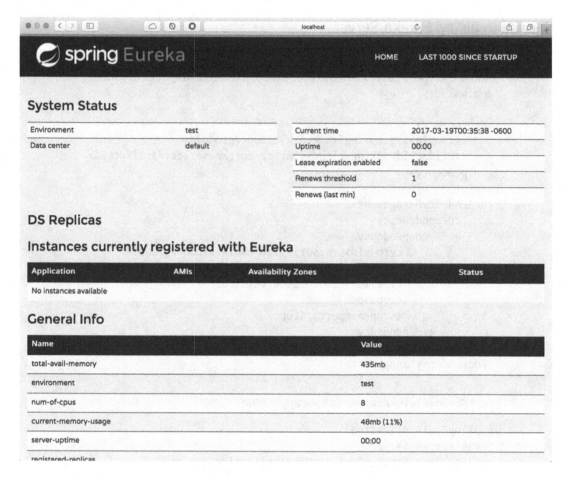

Figure 11-4. *The Eureka server at http://localhost:8761*

3. Add the following properties to application.properties (or
   application.yml):

   ```
   # Default Server Port
   server.port=8761
   ```

   ```
   # Eureka Configuration
   eureka.instance.hostname=localhost
   eureka.client.register-with-eureka=false
   eureka.client.fetch-registry=false
   eureka.client.service-url.defaultZone=http://${eureka.instance.
   hostname}:${server.port}/eureka/
   ```

That's it; you don't need anything else. You can take a look at the service-registry-server-
demo project and run it. It will run in the 8761 port.

Registering a Service Application with the Eureka Server

To register an application, follow these steps:

1. Add the <dependency/> and the <dependencyManagement/> tags to your pom.xml file:

```
<dependency>
    <groupId>org.springframework.cloud</groupId>
    <artifactId>spring-cloud-starter-eureka</artifactId>
</dependency>
...
<dependencyManagement>
    <dependencies>
        <dependency>
            <groupId>org.springframework.cloud</groupId>
            <artifactId>spring-cloud-dependencies</artifactId>
            <version>Camden.SR6</version>
            <type>pom</type>
            <scope>import</scope>
        </dependency>
    </dependencies>
</dependencyManagement>
```

2. Add @EnableDiscoveryClient to your application:

```
@RestController
@SpringBootApplication
@EnableDiscoveryClient
public class ServiceRegistryServiceDemoApplication {

    public static void main(String[] args) {
      SpringApplication.run(
        ServiceRegistryServiceDemoApplication.class, args);
    }

    @GetMapping("/message")
    public String getMessage(){
        return "Hello World from a Service Discovery";
    }
}
```

This annotation will talk to the Eureka server automatically (the default port is 8761).

3. Add the following properties to `application.properties` (or `application.yml`):

```
#Server Port
server.port=8181
```

```
#Application Name
spring.application.name=simple-service
```

It's important to include the application name because that's how it will get discovered.

You can look at the `service-registry-service-demo` project. If you run the application, you should see the name `SIMPLE-SERVICE` listed in the Eureka server. See Figure 11-5.

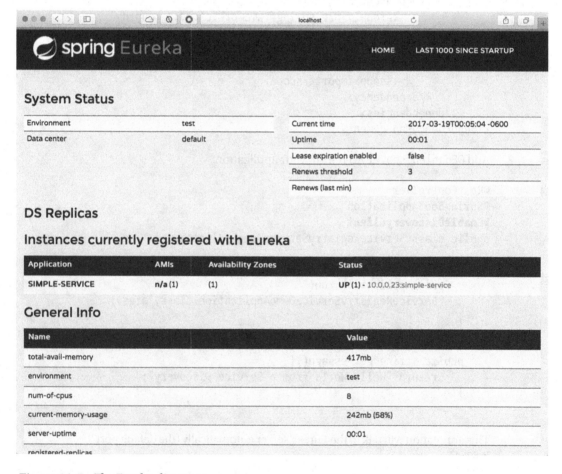

Figure 11-5. *The Eureka discovery*

Accessing the Service Through a Client Application

In order to access the application, follow these steps:

1. Add the <dependency/> and the <dependencyManagement/> tags to your pom.xml file:

```
<dependency>
    <groupId>org.springframework.cloud</groupId>
    <artifactId>spring-cloud-starter-eureka</artifactId>
</dependency>
...
<dependencyManagement>
    <dependencies>
        <dependency>
            <groupId>org.springframework.cloud</groupId>
            <artifactId>spring-cloud-dependencies</artifactId>
            <version>Camden.SR6</version>
            <type>pom</type>
            <scope>import</scope>
        </dependency>
    </dependencies>
</dependencyManagement>
```

2. Use the EurekaClient class and the RestTemplate (in these examples) to get the service.

```
@RestController
@SpringBootApplication
public class ServiceRegistryClientDemoApplication {
    private static Logger log =
        LoggerFactory.getLogger(
                ServiceRegistryClientDemoApplication.class);

    public static void main(String[] args) {
        SpringApplication.run(
            ServiceRegistryClientDemoApplication.class, args);
    }

    private EurekaClient discoveryClient;
    private RestTemplate restTemplate = new RestTemplate();

    ServiceRegistryClientDemoApplication(
                            EurekaClient discoveryClient){
        this.discoveryClient = discoveryClient;
    }
```

```
@GetMapping("/")
public String getMessageFromRemoteServer(){
    return
      restTemplate.getForObject(
            fetchServiceUrl() + "/message", String.class);
    }

private String fetchServiceUrl() {
    InstanceInfo instance = discoveryClient
            .getNextServerFromEureka("SIMPLE-SERVICE", false);
    String serviceUrl = instance.getHomePageUrl();
    log.info(">>> Accessing: " + serviceUrl);
    return serviceUrl;
}

}
```

You can look at the `service-registry-client-demo` project. Here, the EurekaClient uses the getNextServerFromEureka method, passing the name of the service, in this case SIMPLE-SERVICE. (That's why it's important to have an application name in the service.) It does this get a InstanceInfo instance where you can get the actual URL, port, etc., of the service.

Using the Eureka server and the Eureka discovery clients is pretty straightforward. Of course, this is just a simple example, but you can create multiple instances and use a *ribbon* (a client-side load balancer) together with the Eureka server. If you need more information about it, visit http://projects.spring.io/spring-cloud/.

Circuit Breaker

This is an implementation of the *Circuit Breaker pattern*, which prevents cascading failures and provides a fallback behavior until the failing service returns to a normal state. See Figure 11-6.

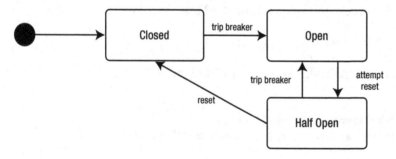

Figure 11-6. *Circuit Breaker pattern*

When you apply a circuit breaker to a service, it watches for failing calls. If these failures reach certain thresholds (which can be set programmatically), the circuit breaker opens and redirects the calls to the specified fallback operation. This gives the failing service time to recover. This pattern implementation is based on Netflix's Hystrix, and the Spring Cloud team enables this feature through annotations. See the following code:

```
@RestController
@SpringBootApplication
@EnableCircuitBreaker
public class CircuitBreakerServiceDemoApplication {

    public static void main(String[] args) {
        SpringApplication.run(
        CircuitBreakerServiceDemoApplication.class, args);
    }

    @Autowired
    private RestTemplate restTemplate;

    @LoadBalanced
    @Bean
    RestTemplate restTemplate() {
        return new RestTemplate();
    }

    @GetMapping("/")
    public String getMessageFromRemoteServer(){
        return this.getMessage();
    }

    @HystrixCommand(fallbackMethod = "defaultMessage")
    public String getMessage(){
        return restTemplate
        .getForObject("http://simple-service" + "/message", String.class);
    }

    public String defaultMessage(){
        return "Nothing here";
    }

}
```

As you can see from this code, it's very simple to use the Circuit Breaker pattern. You just add @EnableCircuitBreaker and @HystrixCommand, passing the fallback method as a parameter. If the service you try to use is not available, it will use the defaultMessage method instead until the service is back up and running.

The Hystrix dashboard can help you monitor your services and get metrics from them. You need to add the spring-boot-actuator and spring-cloud-starter-hystrix-dashboard dependencies to use the dashboard. If you need more information about getting this dashboard, visit http://projects.spring.io/spring-cloud/.

I know there are more services than the Spring Cloud project offers, but those will be for another book. You have now the tools you need to create microservice solutions.

About Reactive Programming

So far I've showed you some Spring services that can be used to meet some of the twelve-factor guidelines and to move toward microservice architectures. This section explains where *reactive programming* fits in to all of this.

Remember that one of the most important features of microservices is the ability to communicate with other microservices, including with legacy systems. Imagine for a moment that your microservice app requires access to several systems at once, and you already have a client that makes several calls to aggregate everything. At some point, this app becomes very chatty (via network latency, concurrency, blocking, etc.) and you don't have only one client making this kind of request. You now have millions of requests. How do you deal with this?

That's where reactive programming enters. It solves this problem using a particular pattern, called an *API Gateway*.

```
Observable<MarketExchangeRates> details = Observable.zip(
  localService.getExchangeRates("usd"),
  yahooFinancialService.getGlobalRates("mxn","jpy"),
  googleFinancialService.getEuropeExchangeRates(),
  (local, yahoo, google) -> {
      MarketExchangeRates exchangeRates = new
                    MarketExchangeRates();
      exchangeRates.setLocalMarket(local.getRates());
      exchangeRates.setEurope(google.getRates({"eur","gpb"}));
      exchangeRates.setGlobal(yahoo.getRate());
      return exchangeRates;
  }
);
```

You can see from the previous code that you can do several tasks in parallel and can avoid resource issues like network hops and latency, concurrency, and blocking. Keep in mind that every service like yahooFinacialService can have a Service Config, can be registered itself to a Service Registry, and can expose default methods in the case of a failure (a circuit breaker).

Summary

This chapter covered the microservices architecture and the challenges you need to face to design native cloud applications.

You learned how Spring Cloud services can help you create fast and easy native cloud applications with the power of Spring Boot, all through messaging. Now you have a better understanding why messaging is important for every architecture and integration solution.

Index

A

Actor Models, 164
Admin processes, 181
Advanced Messaging Queuing Protocol (AMQP)
   bindings, 60
   blocking/unblocking
      events, 76–77
   consumer, 131
   exchanges, 59–60
   integration example, 128, 130
   multi-listeners, 78–79
   producer, 130
   queue, 60
   RabbitMQ (*see* RabbitMQ)
   retries, 79
   transactions, 78
   types of exchanges, 60–61
Aggregator, 113
Annotation-based programming
   model, 173–175
Apache ActiveMQ
   application.properties, 47
   jms-demo application, 49
   queue, 49
   remote broker, 46–50
   reply to, 51–57
      RateSender, 52
   topics, 55–56
Apache Kafka, 134–135
API binder, 135
API Gateway, 192
Application model, 135–136
Aspect-Oriented Programming (AOP), 8
Asynchronous messaging, 2
Async processing, 164

B

Bill of Materials (BOM), 10
Blocking/unblocking events, 76–77
Broker, 1

C

Channel adapters, 113
Circuit breaker pattern, 190–191
Contract patterns, 4
Create, Read, Update and Delete (CRUD), 12
CurrencyController.java class, 13

D

Data-source, 126
Direct exchange, 60
Domain Specific Language (DSL), 114–116

E

Enterprise Integration Patterns: Designing, Building and Deploying Messaging Solutions (book), 111
Eureka server
   register service application, 187–188
   steps, 185–186
@EventListener annotation, 27–28

F, G

Fanout exchange, 61
File integration, 124–128
Functional-based programming model
   HandlerFunctions, 175
   RouterFunctions, 175
   server, 175

© Felipe Gutierrez 2017
F. Gutierrez, *Spring Boot Messaging*, DOI 10.1007/978-1-4842-1224-0

■ H

HandlerFunctions, 175
Headers exchange, 61
Hystrix dashboard, 191

■ I

Integration flow, 114

■ J, K, L

Java Config, 121
Java Message Service (JMS)
    annotations, 42
    Apache ActiveMQbroker (*see* Apache
        ActiveMQ)
    consumer, 38–41
    currency project, 43–46
    jndi.properties, 33
    point-to-point messaging (*see* Point-to-
        point messaging model)
    point-to-point receiver, 33–34
    producer, 36–38
    publish-subscribe messaging (*see*
        Publish-subscribe messaging model)
    rest-api-jms, 57
Java Persistence API (JPA), 8
JDBC integration, 124–128
JSON serialization, 88–92

■ M, N

Message channel patterns, 4
Message-driven pojos (MDPs), 83
Message/messaging
    asynchronous, 2
    channel, 112
    construction patterns, 4
    decoupled, 2
    delivery method, 1
    endpoint, 113
        aggregator, 113
        channel adapters, 113
        filter, 113
        router, 113
        service activator, 113
        splitter, 113
        transformer, 113
    high availability, 2
    interoperability, 2

    models, 3–5
    overview, 1
    patterns, 4–5
    publication, 83
    scalable, 2
    Spring Framework, 5
    Spring Integration, 112
    synchronous, 83
    type patterns, 4
Microservices, 133–134, 162
    cloud-stream-processor-demo, 156–157
    cloud-stream-sink-demo, 157–159
    cloud-stream-source-demo, 155–156
    example, 154
    mobility, 179
    monolith approach *vs.*, 181
    safety, 179
    scalability, 179
    speed, 179
Multiple clients, 111

■ O

Observer pattern, 17–18
    Spring Framework, 18
Opinionated technology, 7, 11

■ P, Q

PING command, 82, 87
Plain Old Java Object (POJO), 115
Point-to-point messaging
        model, 3, 31–32, 112
pom.xml file, 10–11
Port binding, 180
PSUBSCRIBE currency
        command, 82
Publisher commands, 81–82
Publish-subscribe messaging
        model, 3, 32, 34–35, 112, 135

■ R

RabbitMQ, 113, 128, 130–131
    annotations, 69–70
    consumer, 67–68
    features, 62
    flow control, 76
    producer, 63–65, 67
    reply management, 75
    RPC (*see* Remote Procedure Call (RPC))

RabbitMQ Web Management
  processor
    application logs, 150
    changing to text/plain, 151
    exchanges tab, 147
    publish message, 149
    queues tab, 148
    uppercase, 152
  source
    bindings tab, 143
    exchanges tab, 141
    messages, 145
    overview tab, 144
    queues tab, 142
Rate.java Class, 11
RateRepository.java Class, 12
Reactive programming, 163, 192
  async processing, 164
  external service calls, 163
  high concurrent messaging, 163
  reactor, 170
ReactiveX, 164
reactor-demo project, 170–172
REmote DIctionary Server (Redis)
  -cli monitor/subscriber, 91
  commands, 81–82
  message broker, 81–82
  publisher commands, 81–82, 86, 88
  subscriber commands, 81–85
Remote Procedure Call (RPC)
  application, 72
  configuration, 73–74
  request-response
    protocol, 70
  RpcClient, 71
  RpcServer, 72
Rest API currency project
  console logs, 21–22
  custom events, 23–24, 26–27
  URL, 22
RestApiDemoApplication.java Class, 13
rest-api-demo project, 8–9
Restful API
  endpoints, 9
  Spring Boot, 8
RouterFunctions, 175
Routing patterns, 4
RxJava
  -demo project, 164–165, 167, 169–170
  vs. reactor, 173

■ S

Scale, 180
Server Sent Events (SSE)
    technology, 175
Service activator, 113
Service calls, external, 163
Service consumer patterns, 4
Service Provider Interface (SPI), 135
Service Registry
  access application, 189–190
  Eureka server, 185–186, 188
Simple messaging process, 1
Simple/Streaming Text Oriented Message
    Protocol (STOMP), 94
  AnotherController, 104
  application, 107
  browser's developer console, 106
  configuration, 102–103
  RabbitMQ, 108–109
Sink model, 137–138, 153–154, 160
SockJS, 101
Spreadsheets/cells, 163
Spring 5
  WebFlux framework
    annotation-based programming
      model, 173–175
    functional-based programming
      model, 175–176, 178
Spring ApplicationEvent
  events, 18–19
  hierarchy, 18
Spring ApplicationListener, 19–20
Spring Boot
  features, 7–8
  Restful API, 8
Spring Boot Currency Web App
  deploy, 15
  run, 15
Spring Cloud services
  Config Server
    client, 183–184
    cloud, 182–183
    Service Registry, 184–186, 188
Spring Cloud Stream
  application model, 135–136
  applications starters, 160–161
  binder abstraction, 135
  binder API, 135
  consumer groups, 135

Spring Cloud Stream (*cont.*)
    features, 134
    partitioning support, 135
    pom.xml file, 133–134
    processor, 137, 146–150, 152–153
    projects, 133
    publish/subscribe model, 135
    RabbitMQ Web Management, 134, 136,
        140–145
    sink model, 137–138
    source, 137, 139, 141–145
Spring Data Redis module
    publisher, 86, 88
    subscriber, 83–85
Spring Framework, 5
Spring Integration module
    annotations, 118, 120
    file integration, 121–124
    integration annotations, 119
    Java Config, 121
    primer
        message, 112
        message channel, 112
        message endpoint, 113
    usingDSL (*see* Domain Specific
        Language (DSL))
    XML, 116, 118
Spring Tool Suite (STS), 8, 15, 116
StringRedisTemplate class, 86
Subscribe model, 135
Subscriber commands
    code, 84
    MDPs, 83
    Redis interaction with, 82
Synchronous messages, 83

■ T

TCP, 93
Topic exchange, 61
@TransactionalEventListener, 29–30
Transformation patterns, 4
Twelve factor apps
    admin processes, 181
    backing services, 180
    build, release, run, 180
    codebase, 180
    concurrency, 180
    configuration, 180
    cultural, 181
    dependencies, 180
    disposability, 181
    environment parity, 181
    logs, 181
    organizational, 181
    port binding, 180
    processes, 180
    technical, 181

■ U, V

UNIX, 179

■ W

Web archive (WARs), 7–8, 10
WebFlux framework
    annotation-based programming
        model, 173–175
    functional-based programming
        model, 175–176, 178
WebSockets
    CurrencyController, 109
    currency exchange, 110
    low-level
        application, 101
        browser's developer console, 99
        components, 95
        configuration, 95
        handler, 96
        snippet, 96–97
    RateWebSocketsConfig, 109
    STOMP, 94
    TCP, 93

■ X, Y, Z

XML, 116, 118
    channel, 126
    data-source, 126
    query, 126

Get the eBook for only $5!

Why limit yourself?

With most of our titles available in both PDF and ePUB format, you can access your content wherever and however you wish—on your PC, phone, tablet, or reader.

Since you've purchased this print book, we are happy to offer you the eBook for just $5.

To learn more, go to http://www.apress.com/companion or contact support@apress.com.

Apress®